National 4 & 5

History

Free At Last? Civil Rights in the USA 1918–1968

John A. Kerr

HODDER
GIBSON
AN HACHETTE UK COMPANY

The Publishers would like to thank the following for permission to reproduce copyright material:

Photo credits
p.2 DB King; **p.4** (bottom) Piotr Marcinski/Fotolia; **p.6** Library of Congress Prints and Photographs Division; **p.7** (top) Library of Congress Prints and Photographs Division, (bottom) Eldar Kamalov/Wikimedia Commons; **p.8** (left) Anonymous/AP/Press Association Images, (right) AP/Press Association Images; **p.9** Library of Congress Prints and Photographs Division; **p.13** The Ohio State University Billy Ireland Cartoon Library & Museum; **p.14** Courtesy of The Bancroft Library, University of California, Berkeley; **p.15** (bottom) www.CartoonStock.com; **p.16** Wikimedia Commons; **p.17** The Granger Collection/TopFoto; **p.18** (top) Getty Images, (bottom) Bettmann/Corbis; **p.19** An Assembly Line at the Ford Motor Company, c.1910–20 (b/w photo), American Photographer, (20th century)/Private Collection/Archives Charmet/The Bridgeman Art Library; **p.20** Barry Deutsch; **p.21** Wikimedia Commons; **p.22** David J. & Janice L. Frent Collection/Corbis; **p.23** Getty Images; **p.24** Getty Images; **p.27** Time & Life Pictures/Getty Images; **p.29** The Granger Collection/TopFoto; **p.30** (top) Postcard Collection, David M. Rubenstein Rare Book & Manuscript Library, Duke University, (bottom) The Granger Collection/TopFoto; **p.34** Getty Images; **p.35** (top left) Getty Images, (top right) Getty Images, (bottom) Getty Images; **p.36** Getty Images; **p.37** Getty Images; **p.42** Corbis; **p.43** (top) Getty Images; **p.48** Gamma-Rapho via Getty Images; **p.49** Library of Congress Prints and Photographs Division; **p.50** (left) Bettmann/Corbis; **p.54** Getty Images; **p.55** Getty Images; **p.56** (top) Time & Life Pictures/Getty Images, (bottom) Getty Images; **p.59** Getty Images; **p.60** TopFoto/AP; **p.61** (top) Bettmann/Corbis, (bottom) Paris Match via Getty Images; **p.64** The Granger Collection/TopFoto; **p.65** Topham/AP; **p.66** Bettmann/Corbis; **p.69** Found Image Press/Corbis; **p.71** (top) Popperfoto/Getty Images, (bottom) Bill Hudson/AP/Press Association Images; **p.76** Getty Images; **p.77** Popperfoto/Getty Images; **p.81** Bruce Davidson/Magnum Photos; **p.82** Bettmann/Corbis; **p.83** A 1965 Herblock Cartoon, © The Herb Block Foundation; **p.87** Popperfoto/Getty Images; **p.88** Time & Life Pictures/Getty Images; **p.89** Library of Congress Prints and Photographs Division; **p.95** Getty Images; **p.96** Time & Life Pictures/Getty Images; **p.97** BJ/AP/Press Association Images; **p.98** (top) Popperfoto/Getty Images, (bottom) Time & Life Pictures/Getty Images.

Every effort has been made to trace all copyright holders, but if any have been inadvertently overlooked the Publishers will be pleased to make the necessary arrangements at the first opportunity.

Although every effort has been made to ensure that website addresses are correct at time of going to press, Hodder Gibson cannot be held responsible for the content of any website mentioned in this book. It is sometimes possible to find a relocated web page by typing in the address of the home page for a website in the URL window of your browser.

Hachette UK's policy is to use papers that are natural, renewable and recyclable products and made from wood grown in sustainable forests. The logging and manufacturing processes are expected to conform to the environmental regulations of the country of origin.

Orders: please contact Bookpoint Ltd, 130 Park Drive, Abingdon, Oxon OX14 4SE. Telephone: (44) 01235 827720. Fax: (44) 01235 400454. Lines are open 9.00–5.00, Monday to Saturday, with a 24-hour message answering service. Visit our website at www.hoddereducation.co.uk. Hodder Gibson can be contacted direct on: Tel: 0141 848 1609; Fax: 0141 889 6315; email: hoddergibson@hodder.co.uk

© John A. Kerr

First published in 2013 by
Hodder Gibson, an imprint of Hodder Education,
An Hachette UK Company
2a Christie Street
Paisley PA1 1NB

| Impression number | 5 | 4 | 3 | 2 | | |
| Year | 2017 | 2016 | 2015 | 2014 | |

Cover photo: © Paul Schutzer/Time & Life Pictures/Getty Images
Illustrations by Gray Publishing
Produced and typeset in 10/11pt Folio Light by Gray Publishing, Tunbridge Wells
Printed in Dubai

A catalogue record for this title is available from the British Library

ISBN: 978 1444 187 212

Contents

Preface

This is one of a series of six titles for the National 4 & 5 History courses to be assessed from 2014 onwards. Students should study three main units in National 4 & 5 History, with a very wide selection of topics to choose from (five in the first two, ten in the third). The series covers two topics in each unit.

The six titles in the series are:

▶ National 4 & 5 History: Migration and Empire 1830–1939
▶ National 4 & 5 History: The Era of the Great War 1910–1928
▶ National 4 & 5 History: The Atlantic Slave Trade 1770–1807
▶ National 4 & 5 History: Changing Britain 1760–1900
▶ National 4 & 5 History: Hitler and Nazi Germany 1919–1939
▶ National 4 & 5 History: Free at Last? Civil Rights in the USA 1918–1968

Each book contains comprehensive coverage of the four areas of mandatory content for National 5 as well as guidance and practice on assignment writing and assessment procedures.

The Assignment: what you need to know

National 5

What is the assignment for National 5?

The Assignment is an essay written under exam conditions and then sent to the SQA to be marked. It counts for 20 marks out of a total of 80, so doing well in the Assignment can provide you with a very useful launchpad for overall success in the National 5 exam.

What can I write about?

You can write about a question linked to this book or something from another section in the course. In fact, you can write about any historical topic you want. You can even do your Assignment on local history.

What should I write about?

If you decide to do an Assignment based on the content of this book, here are some *good* possible questions:

✓ Why did so many Americans not welcome immigrants after 1918?
✓ Why did the 'Jim Crow' laws and the 'separate but equal' decision cause such problems for black Americans in the 1920s and 1930s?
✓ How important was the Ku Klux Klan in stopping black Americans from gaining civil rights?
✓ How important was Martin Luther King Jr in winning civil rights for black Americans?
✓ To what extent was mass media news reporting important in winning civil rights for black Americans?

What follows are *bad* titles for an Assignment:

✗ Immigration to the USA.
✗ The Ku Klux Klan.
✗ The 'Jim Crow' laws.
✗ Project C in Birmingham.
✗ Martin Luther King Jr.
✗ Black Radicals.

Be safe! There are no prizes for giving yourself a difficult question that you have made up yourself.

Choose something from the history you have already been studying.

Avoid doing something risky – you only get one chance at this assignment.

How long should my Assignment be?

Your assignment has no set length – it is what you can write in 1 hour. Most essays are about four or five pages long.

What skills must I show I am using to get a good mark?

▶ You must choose a question to write about. That means your title should end with a question mark. Don't just write a heading down because you will just start writing a story or a project. Your teacher is allowed to give you a little help to make your choice.
▶ Collect relevant evidence from *at least* two sources of information. For example, these could be two books or one book plus an interview.
▶ Organise and use your information to help answer your question.
▶ Use your own knowledge and understanding to answer the question you have chosen.
▶ Include *at least* two different points of view about your question in your answer.
▶ Write a conclusion that sums up your information and ends by answering the question you started with.

Remember that you also have a Resource Sheet to help you

Your Resource Sheet provides help for you to write your assignment essay.
Your Resource Sheet must show that you have chosen an appropriate title, and researched, selected and organised your information. It shows what sources you have used and how you have used them to reach an appropriate answer to your main question. There is no word limit. The only rule is that all your words must fit on to one side of A4 paper.

Your Resource Sheet will not be marked but it must be sent to the SQA along with your finished essay.

National 4

The Assignment lets you show off your skills as you research a historical issue. You have a lot of choice in what you find out about and you can also choose to present your findings in different ways. That means you don't have to write an essay to show off your skills, knowledge and understanding.

To be successful in National 4 you have to show you can research and use information by doing the following things:

▶ Choosing an appropriate historical theme or event for study. Your teacher can help you choose.
▶ Collecting relevant evidence from *at least two* sources of information.
▶ Organising and using the information that you have collected to help you write about the subject you have chosen.
▶ Describing what your chosen subject is about.
▶ Explaining why your chosen subject happened (its cause) or explaining what happened next because of your chosen subject (its effects).

As you work through this book you will make mobiles, give presentations, and create posters and artwork. All these things could be part of your National 4 assignment. You then have to present your findings.

Don't worry – if you get stuck your teacher is allowed to give you help and advice at *any* stage as you do your Assignment.

Do I have to write a long essay?

No, you don't. You can choose how you present your Assignment. You could do a talk and then be asked some questions about your subject by your teacher. You could do a PowerPoint presentation or keep a learning log or design a poster or other way of displaying your work. You could even write an essay if you wanted to!

Chapter 1 Introduction

What is this course about?

The course starts with a section on immigrants from Europe, why they came to the USA and why it became increasingly more difficult for some immigrants to get into the USA. However, most of the book is about black Americans and their struggle for civil rights.

What will this book help me to do?

This book will help you to be successful in your National 5 and 4 History course. It contains everything you need to know about all the mandatory content and illustrative examples provided by the SQA for 'Free at Last? Civil Rights in the USA 1918–1968'.

The book provides advice and examples to help you answer all the different types of questions you are likely to face in the National 5 exam.

Finally, this book will provide guidance to help you work on the Added Value Assignment tasks.

Why did people go to the USA?

The United States of America is often called 'the land of the free' and 'a land of opportunity'. In the nineteenth and early twentieth centuries people travelled to the USA in the hope of making a better life for themselves and their families.

These **immigrants** believed in the words of the **US Constitution**, the core values of the USA written in 1776, that 'All men are created equal, they are **endowed** by their creator with certain **inalienable** rights, among these are life, liberty and the pursuit of happiness.'

When immigrants travelled to the USA they had made their own version of the US Constitution in their heads. It went something like this: 'Everyone in the USA has the right to get on with their life as they want. Nobody has the right to stop American people from becoming as happy and successful as they want to be and in the way they want to achieve those things.'

Many of the immigrants who flooded into the USA did find happiness and success, but many did not. For some immigrants, and almost all black Americans in the early twentieth century, the USA was not a land of opportunity, nor was it a place to be free.

GLOSSARY

Immigrants people who arrived in a new country to create new lives for themselves

US Constitution the basic rules about how the USA is governed and the rights of American people

Endowed to be given something

Inalienable something that cannot be taken away

When did some immigrants discover that the USA was *not* the land of freedom they expected? Why were their dreams shattered? How and why and when did black Americans gain much greater freedom in their own country?

This book ends with 1968 – was that really a significant year for freedom in the USA? Had all the problems been sorted out? This book is called *Free at Last*? Don't forget the question mark!

The Liberty Bell is an iconic symbol of US independence.

Activity

Stop and think

If you were writing the US Constitution now, how could you set out the same ideas but ensure that everyone was included, no one was excluded and that no group in the country felt offended or uncomfortable with it?

Here are some clues. Do you want to include women and children in this? If it really meant *all* men, then why were Americans happy about keeping and trading slaves? Was this written just for white men? What word would you use for 'inalienable'? What did the original writers mean by 'their creator'? Are you happy to include that idea? What about those who have no religion? It's not so easy!

brotherhood

rights   happiness   Freedom   tranquility

peace   law   property

Some ideas for your constitution.

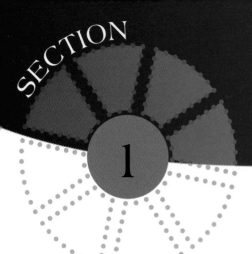

The 'open door' policy of immigration, to 1928

Chapter 2 Different ethnic groups in the USA

What is this chapter about?

The USA had an open door policy towards immigration. This meant that people from all over the world were free to go to the USA to start new lives. By 1900, the USA was a multi-ethnic society. It was hoped that immigrants from different nationalities and cultures would soon lose their old identities and all mix together to become 'Americans'. That was the 'melting pot' idea. In reality, the different ethnic groups did not blend together, perhaps because of prejudice. The dominant group of people in the USA in 1900 were known as Wasps. They were people from north European backgrounds who increasingly feared and disliked the thousands of 'new' immigrants who flooded into the USA after 1900 from southern and eastern Europe.

By the end of this chapter you should be able to:

▶ Describe the feelings and thoughts of new immigrants as they arrived in the USA.
▶ Explain what is meant by the terms 'Wasp', 'melting pot' and the 'American dream'.

The open door policy and immigration

One definition of an American is 'somebody who came from somewhere else to become someone else'. Read that again and take time to think about what it means.

By 1918, the USA was a multi-ethnic society – the **open door** policy meant that anyone could live there. People from all sorts of different cultures lived together in the USA and it was hoped that all those different people would, in time, combine to become 'Americans' sharing a common identity.

A phrase used to describe the idea of people from different backgrounds evolving to share one common identity is the '**melting pot**'. In 1915, US President Wilson said, 'America is like a huge melting pot. We will mix the races together to create a new person – an American.' But did the melting pot really happen?

If you had visited an American city in the early 1900s it would have seemed as if the crowds in the streets were proof that there really was a melting pot. People from all sorts of backgrounds with different cultures and languages were mixing together.

> **GLOSSARY**
>
> **Open door** a policy of allowing anyone to come and live in the USA
>
> **Melting pot** the hope that different nationalities would develop a new identity: an American one

However, if you listened carefully you could have told whether you were in 'Little Italy' or 'Little Russia'.

Immigrants have always tended to live with people who share a similar background, culture and language. By the early 1900s, the thousands of immigrants from southern and eastern Europe felt alone and far from home. They added to the pattern of immigrant housing that was growing in many American cities, where separate communities became identified by names such as 'Little Germany' or 'Irishtown'. As a result, US society in the early twentieth century has been described as a 'salad bowl' where lots of different ingredients, or nationalities, mix together and co-operate but do not lose their separate identities.

Describe as fully as you can what you see in this cartoon on the right. What is the connection between the words on the spoon, the people in the bowl and the woman's skirt? Mortar is another word for cement. What is the stirring figure trying to do? How does this cartoon suggest that, well before 1900, people in America were concerned that not all immigrants were welcome? What point is the cartoonist trying to make?

'The mortar of assimilation – and the one element that won't mix.' A US cartoon from 1889.

What were Wasps?

The USA has always been a land of immigrants. Until the middle of the nineteenth century, most immigrants came from northern Europe, in particular from Britain, Ireland, Germany and Scandinavia. Those 'older' immigrants took pride in how they had defeated the 'Red Indians' (the Native Americans) and made the USA a strong country. They said that the resources of the USA were gifts from God to be used to their advantage. They claimed it was their 'manifest destiny' to develop the USA and keep it safe for their white, Anglo-Saxon, Protestant way of life.

By the end of the nineteenth century, most power in the USA was in the hands of these 'older' immigrants and a new nickname – **Wasp** – was used to describe people descended from immigrants from northern Europe. 'Wasp' stands for White Anglo-Saxon Protestant. The immigrants who were descended from northern Europeans were obviously white, they came originally from a part of northern Europe that is described as Anglo-Saxon and they were mostly Protestant.

US writer F. Scott Fitzgerald shows the attitude of many Wasps in the character of Tom Buchanan in his novel *The Great Gatsby* published in 1925.

I drove over [to Gatsby's mansion] to have dinner with the Tom Buchanans. Daisy [Tom's wife], was my second cousin once removed, and I'd known Tom in college. His family were enormously wealthy in a fashion that rather took your breath away: for instance he'd brought down a string of polo ponies from Lake Forest. It was hard to realize that a man in my own generation was wealthy enough to do that.

'Civilization's going to pieces,' broke out Tom violently. 'I've gotten to be a terrible pessimist about things. Have you read 'The Rise of the Coloured Empires' by this man Goddard?'

'Why, no,' I answered, rather surprised by his tone.

GLOSSARY

Assimilation mixing together to become like everyone else in the USA

Wasp White Anglo-Saxon Protestant

The ideal Wasp – north European, blond, blue-eyed 'Nordic'. If that sounds like Hitler's Aryan master race, wait until you find out about Madison Grant!

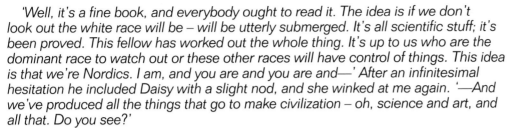

'Well, it's a fine book, and everybody ought to read it. The idea is if we don't look out the white race will be – will be utterly submerged. It's all scientific stuff; it's been proved. This fellow has worked out the whole thing. It's up to us who are the dominant race to watch out or these other races will have control of things. This idea is that we're Nordics. I am, and you are and you are and—' After an infinitesimal hesitation he included Daisy with a slight nod, and she winked at me again. '—And we've produced all the things that go to make civilization – oh, science and art, and all that. Do you see?'

F. Scott Fitzgerald, The Great Gatsby, 1925

Wasp power

Wealthier Wasps liked to think of themselves as the most powerful political and financial ethnic group in the USA.

Most immigrants had no idea about voting or having a say in the way the country was run. The USA was called the land of the free but many immigrants had no clear idea of what political freedom meant. Nor did they know much about how the political system worked. The result of such a lack of knowledge was that many immigrants became followers of any politician who offered them help. These 'helpful' politicians were usually Wasps wanting to attract votes.

New immigrants were amazed when local politicians would help them to get a job or help to get their landlords to repair broken cookers or baths. In bad times, local politicians would help get coal and food and they always knew when a baby was coming and would get a doctor. Never before had new immigrants experienced the power of having a vote!

Immigrant families learned fast and many continued to support certain politicians, mainly because these politicians kept in touch with what the new Americans wanted.

Immigrants also became politically powerful. Later on in this book you will find out about a US president called John F. Kennedy. He was a descendant of Irish Catholics who had emigrated to the USA in the nineteenth century.

In New York city, an organisation called Tammany Hall influenced local politics. It attracted a lot of support from immigrant Irish people by helping immigrants to find jobs and become US citizens, and by assisting the poor.

Real power, however, was still in the hands of politicians, bankers and businessmen (who were mainly Wasps) and they tried very hard to keep it that way.

What were 'new' immigrants and why did they come to the USA?

By the end of the nineteenth century, hundreds of thousands of 'new' immigrants were coming to the USA from the poorer regions of Europe, for example Italy, Poland and Russia. In 1910 the average age of these immigrants was 24.

During the later 1800s, living and working conditions had worsened for millions of Europeans. At the same time, the USA had entered a period of incredible prosperity. After the 1880s, the USA needed more and more unskilled workers to fill the growing number of factory jobs.

People moved for a variety of reasons but all of them could be divided into pull or push reasons.

Pull reasons included hope for a fresh start, good wages and jobs. Cheap land was a huge attraction for poor farm labourers who dreamed of owning their own farms.

Push factors were things in their old lives that immigrants were trying to escape from. Many immigrants were:

▶ Jews who were persecuted and killed in Russia or Poland
▶ Germans who were forced into the army to fight against their wishes
▶ peasants and poor people from across Europe who were forced to pay high taxes or were punished
▶ people who were arrested and tortured in prison just because they had different political or religious ideas.

In the USA, all were free to make their life better, as the cartoon below shows.

'Welcome to all.' A US cartoon from 1880.

Activity 1

Cartoon interpretation

Describe the figure on the extreme left of the 'Welcome to all' cartoon. Who is it meant to be and what does his body language suggest? Try to find out what Bible story this refers to. Why did the artist choose this comparison to make his or her point? List the push reasons you can see in this cartoon that made the immigrants decide to move. List the pull reasons you can see. Look at the areas of colour and light and darkness. Why has the artist used them in this way?

What was the American dream?

All immigrants came to the USA hoping to find a better life, where they would be free and happy. That was, and still is, the **American dream**.

For many Americans, the American dream means the opportunity for anyone, regardless of their background, to become successful if they work hard. The American dream also means equality of opportunity and the chance to 'make good'. A recent example of the American dream is Barack Obama, who became president in 2008. His father came from a poor village in Kenya, and Barack Obama was brought up by his mother in Hawaii, a US state in the middle of the Pacific Ocean.

'Welcome to the land of freedom.' A US drawing from 1887.

Statue of Liberty

The Statue of Liberty was usually the first thing immigrants saw as they approached the USA.

The statue was built in 1886 in New York harbour. It is still an iconic image of the USA and often appears in films symbolising US safety and security.

Many immigrants, when they saw the Statue of Liberty, often broke down in tears of joy. Immigrants such as Jews, who were escaping persecution, were happy at the thought of a free, democratic society. Immigrants escaping hunger and poverty wept with happiness at the thought of riches and an easy life.

One immigrant remembered:

My first impression of the new world will stay with me forever. The steamer taking me from Naples had taken 14 days to reach New York. The ship had 1600 people from Italy. We clustered on the deck, my mother, my stepfather, brother and two sisters and me. We looked in wonder at the miraculous land of our dreams. Mothers and fathers lifted up their babies so they could see the Statue of Liberty. This symbol of America inspired us all. Many older people, remembering the troubles and horrors of what they had escaped from, were openly weeping.

Edward Corsi, In the Shadow of Liberty, 1935.

The statue holds a torch of freedom and the words at the bottom of the statue sum up the reason why many people chose to go to the USA.

'**Give me your tired, your poor,**

Your huddled masses yearning to breathe free,

The wretched refuse of your teeming shore.

Send these, the homeless, tempest-tost to me,

I lift my lamp beside the golden door!'

The Statue of Liberty. The words from a poem 'The New Colossus' by US poet Emma Lazarus are engraved at the bottom of the statue.

Should black Americans be counted as immigrants from a different ethnic background?

The answer is both no and yes, in that order.

Most black Americans are descendants of Africans who were captured and taken to the USA as slaves over the past 400 years. Millions of black Americans lived in the USA around 1900 but very few, if any, were immigrants. Most had been born in the USA, yet for them, America around 1918 was not a free and equal land of opportunity.

In the southern states of the USA, black people were discriminated against by 'Jim Crow' laws and terrorised by the Ku Klux Klan. In the north, they suffered prejudice and discrimination. You will find out a lot more about black Americans in later chapters.

Were 'Red Indians' counted as Americans?

Again, the answer is both yes and no.

By the middle of the nineteenth century, many hundreds of Native American tribes (known as nations) had been wiped out. The US government also had a policy of forcing Native Americans to live on small sections of poor-quality land called reservations, where they were barred from hunting and had to rely on government-issued food rations to survive.

In 1868, the US government had declared that all people who were born in the USA or had become American were citizens of the USA.

However, the government soon ruled that Native Americans were not citizens and could not vote. By 1918, only small improvements in the lives of Native Americans had taken place. It was not until 1924 that Congress declared that all Native Americans born in the USA were citizens.

It should now be clear that by the start of the time period studied in this course, the USA was a multi-ethnic society. However, that does not mean that all racial groups were treated equally, or that they treated each other with respect.

Do you think the person chose to change his appearance? Why might such a change be forced on this Native American?

These photographs show the same person.

Activity 2

1 Choose at least ten words that have been important in this chapter. 'Wasp' is an example. In pairs, play several games of hangman to get used to the spelling of the new words.
2 Summarise this chapter. The following summary reminds you of what this chapter has been about. Words that are important in this chapter have been made into ANAGRAMS. Your task is to sort out the anagrams then write the correct version of this summary into your workbook or work file.

The USA had an **OORD PENO** policy towards immigration, which meant people from all over the world were free to go to America to start new lives. By 1900, the USA was a **ITMUL-NICETH** society. The dominant group of people in the USA in 1900 were known as **SPAWS**. President Wilson hoped that the USA would be like a **TINGMEL TOP** where people from all backgrounds would blend in to become Americans. One group of immigrants who had started going to America many hundreds of years before and felt they were special were **SPAWS**. By the end of the nineteenth century, hundreds of thousands of new immigrants were coming to the USA from poorer regions of Europe such as **TLIAY**, **OPLAND** and **IUSASR**. They were searching for the **ICANAMER EAMDR**.

3 Compare cartoons.

'Where the blame lies.' A US cartoon from 1891.

Compare the 'ark' cartoon on page 6 with the one here. The tall person with the red and white striped trousers is known as Uncle Sam (US) and represents the USA.

▶ In what ways are both cartoons connected?
▶ In what ways are both cartoons taking different points of view?
▶ In the earlier cartoon, list all the positive things that were attracting immigrants to the USA. (A knout was a heavy stick used by law officers to beat people in countries such as Poland. A dungeon is a very dark prison, possibly used for torture.)
▶ In the cartoon above, list all the features that make Uncle Sam look worried.

Do you feel that these cartoons help to show changing attitudes towards immigrants between the 1890s and the 1920s? Give reasons for your answer.

Activity 3

Your challenge!

Your challenge is to draw your own political cartoon about the USA as a multi-ethnic country. It can be about anything at all mentioned in this chapter. Your drawing must be A4 and use at least three colours. It must have a caption of between five and 15 words long. It must be a quality product suitable for display. You have one hour to complete this challenge.

After the class has completed their cartoons, your teacher will display them on a wall. Choose your top three and photograph them with your smartphone. Download the photos into your revision file entitled 'Immigration to America 1900'. If you don't have such a file on your PC, tablet or Mac, start one very soon!

Question practice

National 4

Source A is from the memories of an old immigrant who arrived in New York in 1900.

SOURCE A

The streets of New York were paved with gold – at least it was as good as gold to us. There were markets groaning with food, there was no military on horseback and no whips. To a boy like me it was a giant friendship club.

Describe in your own words what immigrants from Europe felt about life in the USA. You should use Source A and your own knowledge.

Success criteria

Make at least two factual points of information, or one developed piece of information, on what life was like for immigrants in America in 1900.

National 5

1 Describe the attractions of America to new immigrants around 1900. **(5 marks)**

▶ Write five factual pieces of information about the attractions of America to immigrants around 1900, **or**
▶ Write at least three developed pieces of information on the attractions of America to immigrants around 1900.
▶ Give accurate and detailed pieces of information that are properly explained.

There won't be a source in the exam to help you, but to get you started on your answer, use the following clues:

▶ work
▶ food
▶ freedom
▶ American dream.

Source A is from the memories of a Norwegian immigrant who wrote about what he saw in 1910.

SOURCE A

I am on a railroad train winding its way westward between wooded hills for one hundred and fifty miles. I see farms to the right and left with comfortable dwellings and big, red barns, sheltered in groves of planted trees. I see herds of cattle, horses, hogs and sheep browsing on cornstalks left in the fields. I pass through towns with fine buildings for dwellings and business. I remember that Norwegian and Swedish immigrants came here in canvas-covered wagons pulled by oxen and out of the wilderness made what I now see. How proud they well may be of that hard, creative work!

2 Evaluate the usefulness of Source A as evidence of the experience of immigrants to America in 1910. (You may want to comment on who wrote it, what type of source the extract is taken from such as a letter or newspaper report or a diary, when it was written, why it was written, what information is in it or what has been missed out.) **(6 marks)**

▶ To get a mark, you need to explain the importance of each of the points you make about the source.
▶ Up to 4 marks may be given for points about who wrote it, what type of source the extract is taken from, when it was written and why it was written.
▶ Up to 2 marks can be given for your comments about how useful the content of the source is in terms of the question.
▶ Up to 2 marks can be given for your comments about what the source does not tell us. In other words, what would have made the source more useful had the extra information been included.

Chapter 3 Changing attitudes to immigrants after 1918

What is this chapter about?

Even before 1918, many Americans were becoming more and more concerned with the millions of 'new' immigrants arriving in the USA from the poorer areas of Europe. When the First World War ended in 1918, there was a concern that the USA would be flooded by millions of new immigrants. Those fears added to other concerns about immigrants so that during the 1920s, new laws were passed to limit the number of immigrants coming to the USA. The open door started to close.

By the end of this chapter you should be able to:

▶ Explain why attitudes towards immigrants changed around 1918.
▶ Describe what was done to limit immigration to the USA in the 1920s.

Why did attitudes towards immigrants start to change?

Many Wasps were afraid that the arrival of new immigrants from southern and eastern Europe would threaten their way of life. This fear of immigrants, who were in some ways different from the older 'Wasp' immigrants, led to demands to close the 'open door', at least to immigrants from poorer, non-Wasp countries.

Many of the new immigrants were Jewish or Catholic, and looked very different from the more traditional immigrants from northern Europe.

During most of the nineteenth century, American leaders felt that immigration helped the US economy. Businessmen were happy to see waves of immigrants arriving to provide cheap labour for their factories. However, businessmen began to change their minds as trade unions grew larger and more powerful and strikes became more common. Americans thought that immigrants from countries like Russia were the cause of strikes and riots. In the late 1890s, an American businessman wrote:

The problems which confront us to-day are serious enough without being complicated and made worse by the addition of millions of Hungarians, Italians, Poles and Russian Jews.

Francis A. Walker, The Atlantic Monthly, *June 1896*

A US cartoon, 'The stranger at our gate.'

Activity 1

Cartoon interpretation

Look at the gatepost in the cartoon above and read the words on it. Why has the immigrant arrived at the entrance to the USA? How can you tell that the American figure does not like the new arrival? How does the cartoonist make the new immigrant seem very unpleasant (look at his appearance and read all the words). What message is the cartoonist trying to give about 'new' immigration?

CHING HI
WASHEE MAN

A US cartoon from The Chinese in California, 1850–1925.

However, for some immigrants, the open door had already closed before 1900 when the USA had cut Oriental or Asian immigration. The first powerful law restricting immigration into the USA was the Chinese **Exclusion** Act of 1882. Chinese immigration was made illegal in 1902.

In 1907, the Japanese government promised to stop the emigration of its citizens to the USA. During the nineteenth century, thousands of Chinese and Japanese had emigrated to the USA, many helping to build the railways. By 1900, they were a popular target as the above cartoon shows.

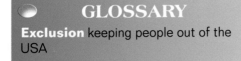

GLOSSARY

Exclusion keeping people out of the USA

Why did the open door start to close?

Until about 1890, the millions of immigrants who settled in the USA came mostly from Britain, Ireland, Germany, Scandinavia and from other countries in north-western Europe. It was not until the early twentieth century that the majority of immigrants came from countries such as Turkey, Italy or Greece in south-eastern Europe.

In 1907, the US government wanted to know more about the 'problem of immigration' so it set up the Dillingham Commission. The Dillingham Commission discovered that, since the 1880s, immigrants had come mainly from southern and eastern Europe. The Commission thought that immigrants from places like Austria-Hungary, Russia, Italy, Turkey, Lithuania, Romania and Greece were inferior compared to the Wasp-type immigrants who had come before 1890.

The Commission recommended that literacy tests be used to make it harder for 'inferior immigrants' to get into the USA. In other words, if an immigrant could not read or write English he or she would find it difficult to get into the USA. However, many thousands of immigrants still arrived in the USA.

'The unrestricted dumping ground', a cartoon from 1903. It shows the fear of immigrants bringing political ideas such as socialism and anarchism to the USA. There are also fears about organised crime (the Mafia) shown here. All these problems are, according to the cartoonist, imported 'direct from the slums of Europe daily'.

What do you think Uncle Sam is thinking in the cartoon above? How are the immigrants shown? Why did the cartoonist choose to represent them this way? How does the title show the attitude of the cartoonist? What do you think the cartoonist wanted to happen to immigrants? Give reasons for your answer.

GLOSSARY

Anarchism the destruction of all government, law and order

Mafia organised crime gangs that began in Sicily, Italy

A modern cartoon.

Why did US attitudes become harder against immigrants after 1918?

Americans blamed many of their country's problems on the new immigrants. The answer to the USA's problems seemed to be to stop immigration, especially from 'undesirable' parts of the world. It was as if the words on the Statue of Liberty had lost their meaning (look back to page 7).

Many Americans feared revolution

In 1917, revolution turned Russia into a communist state. **Communism** is a political ideology that is the exact opposite of the US political system. As many thousands of immigrants to the USA came from Russia and eastern Europe, the US authorities began to fear that the immigrants would bring communist ideas with them and perhaps start a revolution there as well. That fear was called the '**red** scare'. The word 'red' was used to mean communist. At the time, anarchists or communists in the USA made up only 0.1 per cent of the overall population.

> ### GLOSSARY
> **Communism** a political belief that society should be classless, which sparked off the Russian revolution
> **Red** Communist
> **Bolshevism** Communism

This was also a time of protests and strikes as trade unions tried to get better conditions for their members. In 1919 there was a huge wave of strikes in the USA. There was a nationwide strike of steelworkers. The strikers were often unskilled and semi-skilled workers, many of whom were recent immigrants from southern and eastern Europe. People against the trade unions wasted no time in linking the union strikes with the spread of **Bolshevism**. Anti-union voices blamed all strikes on red secret agents, who were entering the USA disguised as immigrants.

The US film industry was very influential even before 1918. In films such as *The Dynamiters* released in 1911, socialist and Bolshevik men were shown as eastern Europeans with wild hair, straggly beards and bulging eyes that shone with madness. These foreigners were always shown with a fist punching the air and at some point in the movie they were seen throwing bombs.

'Come unto me, ye opprest.' A US cartoon from 1919. The word 'anarchist' means someone who is opposed to most forms of government. Today, such a person would be called a terrorist.

The red scare was made worse by the terrorist activities of small revolutionary groups inside the USA such as the Wobblies – the Industrial Workers of the World (IWW). Members of the IWW had been found guilty of murder by bombing as early as 1906, so imagine how film-goers would be frightened by movies that suggested the USA was under terrorist threat.

When US Attorney General Mitchell Palmer's house in Washington, DC, was blown up and letter bombs were sent to government officials, the public's fears of violent red revolution seemed to be confirmed.

When a wave of strikes broke out in 1919, thousands of socialists, communists and IWW supporters were arrested, jailed or deported because of their political beliefs. The red scare reached a peak of hysteria in January 1920 when, one night, Palmer ordered the arrest of 4000 alleged communists in 33 cities. A panic had set in that if the workers in Russia could take control there, what was to prevent revolutionary workers in the USA trying for revolution here too? New immigrants were coming from communist areas and had been for a long time. Was it not time to stop them coming?

'Put them out and keep them out.' A US newspaper cartoon from 1919.

When it became clear that there was no risk of revolution in the USA, the red scare faded away – but not before it increased suspicion of immigrants.

Americans feared that immigrants brought more crime

In the early 1920s, crime was increasing and many US politicians chose to blame immigrants. Crime had existed in the USA since its very beginning, and organised gangs had operated in New York and other cities for many years. However, the newspapers of the time now had a new word to play with – Mafia. The Mafia is a name for organised crime gangs who originated in Sicily, Italy. Naturally, as thousands of Italians emigrated to the USA, the Mafia became established there also.

Another development after the First World War was an increased dislike of both Italian and German immigrants.

The US government believed that drinking alcohol was a bad thing. The Volstead Act of 1919 banned the sale of all alcohol. This was called **prohibition**. Banning the sale of alcohol is one thing, but it did not stop people wanting to drink it, so the organised crime gangs stepped in to supply the 'booze'. In the minds of the public, a strong connection was made between crime and the organised crime gangs of Italian immigrants.

> ### GLOSSARY
> **Prohibition** a time in the 1920s when the USA tried to ban the sale of all alcohol

One of the most famous names to link immigrants to crime and illegal alcohol was Alphonse Gabriel 'Al' Capone. He was an American gangster who led the Chicago Outfit, which became known as the 'Capones'. Based in Chicago from the early 1920s to 1931, it was dedicated to smuggling and transporting alcohol, and other illegal activities such as prostitution.

Capone was born in New York city but his parents were Italian immigrants. Capone represented the fear and dislike that many Americans had of the Mafia and reinforced the stereotype that all Italian immigrants were in some way linked to crime.

Why is the trial of Sacco and Vanzetti important?

Ferdinando Nicola Sacco and Bartolomeo Vanzetti were suspected anarchists convicted of murdering two men during an armed robbery at a shoe factory in 1920. After a controversial trial and a series of appeals, the two Italian immigrants were executed on 23 August 1927. Since their deaths, most people now feel that the two men were convicted largely on their anarchist political beliefs and did not kill anyone. It is now felt that Sacco and Vanzetti just 'fitted the frame'. Many Americans felt that the two men would be found guilty, not because they were guilty of the robbery and murder, but because they were immigrants and had strong **radical** ideas about changing the US political system. A radical is someone who has fairly extreme political beliefs but it does not necessarily mean that they support violence.

The trial began in July 1921. Public opinion was divided: some Americans believed that anyone who wanted to change the whole of the USA's political system was already guilty and should be hanged. Others believed that in a democracy all people should be free to believe what they want. Because of protests both at home and abroad, the trial dragged on for six years.

Al Capone photographed in 1930.

GLOSSARY
Radical wanting fast change, sometimes with violence

Worldwide protests supported Sacco and Vanzetti. This photograph was taken in London. Recent forensic tests prove beyond doubt that Sacco's gun was used in the murder.

In his final statement on 7 April 1927, Vanzetti claimed that the trial had not been about murder, but rather his political ideas and where he came from:

I am suffering because I am a radical. Indeed I am a radical. I have suffered because I was an Italian. Indeed, I am an Italian.

The trial of Sacco and Vanzetti received nationwide publicity and, rightly or wrongly, it tended to remind Americans of the connection between immigrants and crime.

Did immigrants make houses and jobs harder to get for Americans?

Housing

In the north-east of the USA, in and around New York, the large numbers of immigrants did make life harder for working-class Americans who already found their lives difficult enough.

The great majority of new immigrants settled in cities where they could only afford to live in slum housing. Newly arrived immigrants tended to cluster in areas where other immigrants who shared the same culture had already settled. As a result, areas of north-eastern cities came to be known as 'Little Italy' or 'Little Poland' because of the people who settled there.

The poor conditions in which they lived were a very serious problem for many immigrants. These slums became centres of disease and crime and they got worse as more people, including the rural poor, arrived looking for cheap housing. Landlords knew that high demand meant they could raise rents without necessarily improving the quality of their housing. As a result, the white working-class residents also saw their rents being forced up and housing became harder to find because of competition from immigrants.

> **GLOSSARY**
>
> **Assembly line** factory work where workers only do one simple task in a long process

Jobs

In the early 1900s, new ways of working in factories were being introduced which sped up the production of many things. By using **assembly line** methods, the need for skilled workers was reduced. Factory owners realised that they could make larger profits while at the same time employing immigrants and paying them lower wages. Suddenly, skilled workers in factories saw their jobs threatened by competition from new immigrants. Of course, it was not the fault of the immigrants, but nevertheless dislike of immigrants increased.

At the same time as immigration was increasing, trade union members were trying to get better wages and working conditions. When the union members campaigned to improve conditions, for example by going on strike, they found that their bosses simply sacked them and replaced them with immigrants.

An Assembly Line of the Ford Motor Company

The job of the man on the bottom right is to turn a wheel. That's all. Suddenly factories did not need skilled engineers. An immigrant worker could be shown what to do in less than five minutes.

In the strikes that swept the USA in 1919, new immigrants were used as 'strike breakers'. Italian, Polish or Russian immigrants were prepared to work longer hours for lower wages than their fellow American workers. After all, they were still able to earn more than would have been possible back home in their 'old country'. As the resentment towards immigrant strike breakers and rising rents increased, so did the desire to stop immigrants coming into the USA.

Nativism and racism

New immigrants also faced prejudice and discrimination from Americans who saw them as a threat to the 'American way of life'. Those fears were most common in 'small-town America', a description of not only a place but also a state of mind.

Many of the Americans who lived in small towns and communities felt under threat. They believed that their religious beliefs, social customs and democratic political system – in fact their whole way of life – was under threat from mass immigration. The following cartoon suggests that **nativism** is alive and well today!

> ### GLOSSARY
> **Nativism** a belief that ideas and people from outside the USA were bad

Why is this cartoon sitting beside text about nativism? What are the core ideas of nativism? How does the cartoonist feel about nativism? How would you feel if you lost your job or your house because your boss hired immigrant workers? Fecundity means people having too many children. Can people have too many children? Does this activity tell us anything about the relationships of people from different backgrounds living and working together?

'History marches on; nativism marches in place.' A modern US cartoon.

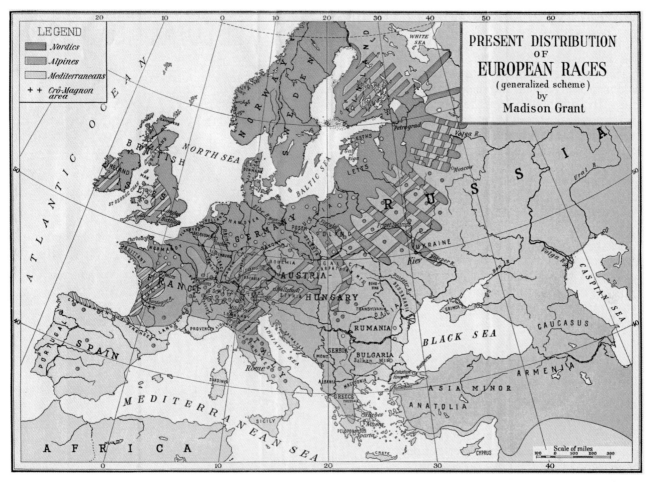

A map from Grant's book. Grant argued that only those people from the red areas (Nordics) should be allowed to settle and breed in the USA. People from the green and yellow areas were inferior and should be banned.

'Nativism' is another word for small-town values and intense dislike of foreigners. It was most common in the mid-western and southern states. In those 'Bible belt' areas, conservative ideas were popular. People there often believed that the Bible was literally true and that new ideas, even new scientific ideas such as the theory of evolution, were sinful. Nativists believed that immigrants brought new and sinful ideas into the USA, so they should be stopped from entering the country. Nativists also claimed to have scientific evidence to support their dislike of immigrants.

In 1916, Madison Grant published a book called *The Passing of the Great Race*. Grant argued that the 'new immigrants' were inferior to the older type of immigrants. Grant was a racist who believed that people from northern Europe (**Nordics**) were better than other races.

A new science called **eugenics** (said as *U-jen-iks*) claimed to prove that some races were inferior to others. Grant even argued that people from those areas who were already settled in the USA should undergo **sterilisation** to prevent them having 'inferior' children.

Grant gained a lot of support from people who wanted a strong eugenics policy to save 'Nordics' from being swamped by other races entering the USA after 1918. There is strong similarity between Grant's beliefs and Hitler's ideas of an Aryan master race. Hitler even said that Madison Grant's book was one of his favourites.

> ### GLOSSARY
> **Nordics** people from northern Europe
>
> **Eugenics** a belief that one race of people is genetically better than another
>
> **Sterilisation** a medical procedure to stop women from being able to have children. Sometimes done against the will of the woman

Why did the Ku Klux Klan revive around 1915?

The Ku Klux Klan (KKK) was reinvented in 1915 as a direct response to growing fears of immigrants arriving with 'un-American' ideas. The original KKK was formed in the late 1860s and was known as an organisation that persecuted black Americans. However, from 1915 the KKK tapped into the fears of small-town USA and declared it would protect Wasp Americans from Catholics, Jews and any foreign influence the Klan thought was 'un-American'. In fact, the new slogan of the Klan by 1920 was 'America for Americans'.

By the early 1920s, the KKK was described as *the* social organisation for white, Protestant Americans. Many Wasps welcomed the Klan into their churches, their homes and their lives. You can find out more about the Klan on pages 34–40.

Did the First World War affect attitudes towards immigrants?

Yes, it did. The propaganda against Germans has already been mentioned.

A large part of the US immigrant population was of German or Austrian origin, but during the war the US public were persuaded that Germany was an enemy of the USA. Propaganda stories reported German atrocities during the war. Although some of those stories were made up, the US public came to resent and dislike immigrants from Germany and the old Austrian Empire.

A Ku Klux Klan songbook published in the 1920s.

City streets in Chicago with German names were changed, and the city of Berlin, Michigan was renamed Marne. The German food sauerkraut came to be called 'liberty cabbage', German measles became 'liberty measles', hamburgers became 'liberty sandwiches' and Dachshunds became 'liberty pups'. Many families with a German-sounding last name changed their surname.

A second anti-German connection was made by people wanting to stop immigration. Many Germans were involved in the brewing industry (even today, Schlitz and Budweiser are popular brands that were originally made by German brewers) and if alcohol was a threat to the US way of life, then it stood to reason Germans were a bad influence too! Anti-immigration groups had found another way to stir up feeling against immigrants.

Finally, during the war, many Americans resented having to become involved in Europe's problems. After all, most of them had chosen to leave Europe's problems behind when they left for the USA. When the war ended, the US government chose to become isolationist. That meant it wanted nothing to do with any problems outside the USA. For that reason, many US citizens did not want fresh waves of immigrants bringing 'European' problems to the USA.

What is the purpose of the poster? Is this an effective poster? What effect would propaganda like this have on attitudes to future immigration?

A military recruitment poster from 1917. Look closely at the poster and you will see the English word 'enlist' and just above that, where the 'Mad Brute' is standing, you can see 'America' written on the land.

How did the USA close its open door and start to restrict immigration?

So far you have been looking at reasons to explain *why* the open door policy ended in the USA. This section is about *how* the door was closed.

By 1921, the US government took its first steps towards closing the open door for immigrants. A quota system only allowed a limited number of immigrants into the country. Every ten years, most governments count how many people live in a country. That count is called a census. The US government knew from its 1910 census how many people of different nationalities lived in the USA. The government then announced that only a further three per cent of each nationality already in the USA would be allowed to come into the USA. For example, if there had been 1000 people who had emigrated from Malta, then only a further three per cent from Malta (in total 30 people) would be allowed into the USA.

The government soon realised it had made a mistake. By using the 1910 census it was accepting that many thousands of 'new' immigrants could get into the USA.

New restrictions in 1924 lowered the proportion from each country to two per cent, based on the sizes of national groups in the USA at the time of the 1890 census – when there were far fewer 'new' immigrants living in the USA. By changing the rules the US government would not have to allow so many immigrants in from southern and central Europe!

Both the 1921 and the 1924 Immigration Acts discriminated unfairly against people who were not from western Europe. People from southern, central and eastern Europe found it harder to emigrate to the USA.

By 1929, it became even harder to gain entry to the USA. Only 150,000 immigrants a year were allowed to enter the USA and 85 per cent of that number were reserved for immigrants from northern and western Europe. When President Coolidge declared that 'America must be kept American', he meant that new immigration laws should limit the number of immigrants from southern and central Europe and allow in more from the traditional areas of northern and western Europe.

By 1930, immigration from southern and eastern Europe and Asia had almost stopped.

In 1932, Franklin Roosevelt, the man who was about to become the next US president, summed up the reasons why the USA no longer had an open door policy:

Our last frontier has long since been reached … There is no safety valve in the form of a Western prairie … We are not able to invite immigration from Europe to share our endless plenty.

Activity 2

Once you have read the text on pages 23–4, make a sketch of this cartoon. Label at least seven features that you can see in the image that are relevant to immigration restriction.

'Uncle Sam's quota.' A US cartoon from 1921.

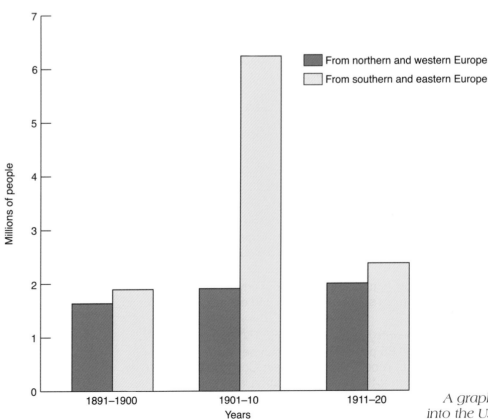

A graph showing immigration into the USA from 1890 to 1920.

Activity 3

Interpreting the statistics

Look at the graph on page 24 and answer the following questions.

1 True or false?
   ▶ Old immigration was higher than new immigration only after 1900.
   ▶ New immigration was higher than old immigration in every decade between 1891 and 1920.
   ▶ The highest number of new immigrants was between 1911 and 1920.
   ▶ The highest number of new immigrants was between 1901 and 1910.

2 Why do you think immigration fell so much between 1911 and 1920? (Clue: First World War.)

3 By looking at the pattern of migration and the answer you gave to question 2, what would you predict as a likely figure for old and new immigration from 1921 onwards?

4 Why might your prediction for the 1920s make you think carefully about the open door policy for immigrants?

Activity 4

Project task

Make a hanging mobile. Your mobile should illustrate the reasons why anti-immigration ideas grew in the USA after 1918. You can choose to work on your own or as part of a group of no more than four people. If you work in a group, you must also design and use a creativity log in which you record exactly what each person in the group contributed to the final mobile.

Success criteria

▶ Your mobile must have at least five strands.
▶ Each strand should be about a main reason for changing attitudes towards immigrants.
▶ Each strand should have several mobile items attached.
▶ Each strand must have two text items, perhaps only one significant name or word summarising the reason.
▶ Each strand must have at least one large double-sided illustration linked to the reason.
▶ Each strand must have a three-dimensional feature linked to the reason.
▶ Your mobile should hang easily.
▶ Your mobile must be clearly seen and read from a distance.
▶ Each mobile must be attractive, colourful and relevant to the project task.

Question practice

Source A is about US attitudes to immigrants in 1920.

SOURCE A

People thought America must be kept pure and not turned into a second-rate power by second-rate people. By the 1920s several laws had restricted the flow of immigrants to the USA. Only so many immigrants from each country were allowed in to the USA.

Explain in your own words what the source tells us about US attitudes to immigrants in 1920. You should use Source A and your own knowledge.

Success criteria

In your answer you should make at least two points of information about attitudes to immigrants.

National 5

Source A was written in 1918 by a person whose family had settled in in the USA 50 years earlier.

SOURCE A

The USA should no longer be open to just any foreigner. These new immigrants cannot read or write and many have no money. We true Americans want to look after ourselves first of all. We don't want our jobs and homes taken away from us by immigrants. There are far too many people coming from southern Europe and many are Catholic or Jewish. They are not good Protestants like us.

Evaluate the usefulness of Source A as evidence about the changing attitudes towards immigrants to the USA before 1928. **(5 marks)**

You need to make five clear points about the usefulness of the source. You would probably start by arguing that the source does provide useful evidence about immigration.

You could mention:

▸ The source was written in 1918 at a time when immigration to the USA was increasing.
▸ It was written to explain why the author supports immigration restriction.
▸ It claims that immigrants cannot read or write.
▸ It claims that immigrants are poor.
▸ It claims that immigrants will take away jobs and homes.
▸ It claims that old immigrants should be looked after first.

You could decide, however, that in some ways the source is less useful because:

▸ The source was written by an American who was not a new immigrant therefore possibly biased.
▸ Important information has not been mentioned.
▸ Wasps had developed a strong resentment of new immigrants.
▸ It fails to mention that literacy tests had already been imposed.
▸ Immigrants often took jobs which others did not want.
▸ Americans were also afraid of increasing crime, possible revolution and immigrants undermining the 'American way of life'.

Chapter 4 The 'Jim Crow' laws

What is this chapter about?

Slaves were set free in 1865 after the US Civil War had ended, but very quickly new ways of controlling the black population of the South were started. One method was by using 'Jim Crow' laws which segregated blacks from whites. These laws denied black Americans their freedom. In 1896, the Supreme Court of the USA reached a decision about the laws. The court stated that segregation in the USA (and therefore 'Jim Crow' laws) was legal and did not treat black Americans unfairly. As a result, 'Jim Crow' segregation laws continued in the USA for almost another 60 years.

By the end of this chapter you should be able to:

▶ Explain why 'Jim Crow' laws were started in the South after the US Civil War.
▶ Describe how 'Jim Crow' laws helped to create a segregated society.

Freedom?

In 1863, US President Abraham Lincoln declared that slavery was illegal and that slaves were now free. In 1963, Martin Luther King Jr stood on the steps of the memorial to Abraham Lincoln and gave his 'I Have a Dream' speech in which he hoped that one day his four small children would be judged by the content of their character rather than the colour of their skins.

Why had 100 years passed since slaves were meant to be free yet clearly they were not 'free at last'? The main reason lay in the refusal of the white society, mainly in the southern states of the USA, to allow black Americans to become free and equal citizens.

Why 1865 was a turning point for black Americans – or was it?

Before 1865, most black Americans in the southern states of the USA were slaves. The white owners of slaves could buy and sell their slaves at any time. Slave families could be split up without warning. Most slaves worked on plantations. Plantations were large farms that produced mostly cotton or tobacco. Plantation owners argued that if slavery were to be abolished, the plantations would be ruined. Most of these plantations were in the southern states of the USA. A more common description for the southern states of the USA is the 'South'.

The US Civil War was fought between the North and the South between 1861 and 1865. One of the reasons for the war was the question of slavery. The northern states – the North – did not want slavery. The southern states – the South – did. When the North won the Civil War in 1865 it looked as if black people would be 'free at last'.

Although he is smiling in the picture, what words could you list to describe his real feelings as he got ready to make the speech? Why do you think he chose this location for his famous 1963 speech?

This is Martin Luther King Jr standing in front of the Lincoln Memorial.

Black Americans were even more hopeful of a better life in 1868 when a change was made to the US Constitution (a word for a set of rules which says how the USA should be governed), which said that black people had the right to freedom and to be treated by law in the same way as white people. In 1870 another change to the Constitution, officially called the fifteenth **amendment**, gave black American adult males the right to vote.

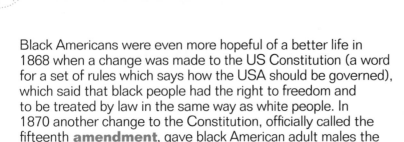

The fifteenth amendment also said that nobody should lose their right to vote because of their colour or race.

It seemed for a short time after the Civil War that the life of the USA's former slaves would improve. However, by 1900 almost no black person in the South was able to vote easily, '**Jim Crow**' laws restricted the freedoms of black Americans and the Supreme Court decision of 1896 denied most black Americans the freedom they thought they had won in the 1860s.

Why couldn't black Americans vote when they had been given the right to vote in 1870?

To be able to vote in the USA it was necessary to be registered. Many southern states created new voting rules which made it very difficult for black Americans to register. Some examples of these voting qualifications included literacy tests, the ability to understand and explain complicated rules about the government, and the introduction of a tax that had to be paid before registering to vote. There were places, especially in the North, where black voters did elect black representatives and senators but the reality was that most black Americans in the South did not vote because white society made it difficult for them to do so. In 1900 there were 180,000 black people with the right to vote in Alabama. When that state made it difficult for black Americans to register to vote, the number of actual voters fell to 3000.

Why was difficulty in voting a serious problem for black Americans?

By 1900 very few black people in the South were able to vote. If they could not vote, they could not elect politicians to fight against 'Jim Crow' laws. Politicians in the South relied on white voters. Since many of the white voters were also racist, it made no political sense to campaign to help black people in the South. It also made no sense for politicians to even try to stop the torture and murder of black Americans that was known as 'lynching'. Even Woodrow Wilson, who was president in 1918, described black Americans as 'an ignorant and inferior race'.

Why did problems increase for black Americans after the Civil War?

When slaves were slaves, everyone knew what was expected of them. Black slaves could be punished if their owner did not like what the slave said, did or even the way they looked. Once slaves were freed, the white population of the South worried how they could continue to control their former slaves. There were two answers: 'Jim Crow' and the Ku Klux Klan.

Who or what was Jim Crow?

The South was determined to keep control over the black population. They made new laws in their own states called 'Jim Crow' laws. The name Jim Crow is not any one person, it is just a nickname for all sorts of laws that treated black Americans unfairly, that made sure black and white people were kept separate and that black people were denied their legal rights.

The name Jim Crow seemed to start as a silly dancing character that appeared in stage shows across the South. The Jim Crow character was developed by a performer known as Thomas Dartmouth 'Daddy' Rice, a white man who darkened his face with burnt cork , dressed in baggy clothes and danced a silly jig while reinforcing Southern beliefs that black people were inferior to whites. The name Jim Crow caught on and was being used to describe segregated railroad carriages as early as the 1840s, long before the Civil War even started.

The southern states used 'Jim Crow' laws to maintain a segregated society in which white authority kept control over the black population.

Many white southerners said that **segregation** just meant that black and white people would have **separate but equal** facilities. Most black people disagreed with the 'separate but equal' claim. They agreed that 'Jim Crow' laws kept the races apart but black Americans claimed that places as different as cinemas, toilet facilities and railway carriages were seldom separate and equal.

The following description was written by a modern-day historian:

The realities of Jim Crow were harsh. Wherever black people lived or travelled in the South they were faced with the humiliation of seeing doors that were open to white people legally closed to them: restaurant and motel doors, movie house doors … the public parks, pools, beaches … were all closed. Or they would find two sets of doors, two kinds of facilities from drinking fountains to schools. One set of doors was white the other was black, one set was clean and well cared for … the other was usually broken, neglected by the white authorities, shamefully unequal.

> By looking at the picture, do you agree that Rice and his stage act were harming black people in some way?

GLOSSARY

Segregation keeping black and while people apart

Separate but equal a phrase used in a decision of the Supreme Court in 1896 that made segregation legal and respectable across the USA

A drawing of 'Daddy' Rice performing his Jim Crow dance. The text below this picture states, 'Thomas Dartmouth "Daddy" Rice … reinforced southern beliefs that black people were inferior to whites.'

A racist postcard.

What point do you think the cartoonist was trying to make about the lives of black Americans at the end of the nineteenth century? If you were about to use this cartoon in a book you were writing, what words would you put in the speech bubble?

'Jim Crow' laws affected every part of a black American's life. Black children were forbidden to attend school with white children. Black Americans had only restricted access to public places such as parks and restaurants. At work they had separate bathrooms and collected their pay separately from whites. There were strict bans on whites and blacks marrying and cemeteries even had to provide separate graveyards.

The situation was made even worse by a decision of the Supreme Court in 1896.

What did the Supreme Court decide in 1896?

The Supreme Court is the most important legal court in the USA. It does not *make* laws, it makes *decisions*. The Supreme Court decides if any law takes away or limits the basic rights of people that are guaranteed in the US Constitution. In 1896, the Supreme Court made a decision about a legal case involving a black man called Homer Plessy.

In 1892, Plessy objected to having to move from his seat on a train just because it was reserved for white people. Plessy was arrested and found guilty under the 'Jim Crow' laws. Plessy, however, was a determined man and fought his case through more and more important legal courts in the USA. Eventually, the case went to the Supreme Court. Plessy argued that the 'Jim Crow' laws broke federal law and were against the US Constitution.

How does this photo show a flaw in the Supreme Court's belief that separate but equal was a fair idea?

A vending machine in a shop from the 1940s. How does this photo show that 'separate but equal' continued long after 1896?

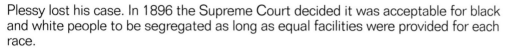

Plessy lost his case. In 1896 the Supreme Court decided it was acceptable for black and white people to be segregated as long as equal facilities were provided for each race.

The decision, or ruling, of the Supreme Court was called the 'separate but equal' decision. It accepted that 'Jim Crow' laws were legal and acceptable across the USA. Mainly as a result of this ruling, segregation was strengthened and did not start to break down until 1954, nearly 60 years in the future.

Activity 1

Summarise this chapter

The following summary reminds you of what this chapter has been about. Words that are important in this chapter have been made into ANAGRAMS. Your task is to sort out the anagrams then write the correct version of this summary into your workbook or work file.

ERYSLVA was **EDBOLAISH** after the US Civil War ended in **5681**. After the Civil War, states in the **THSOU** began to make laws that treated black Americans unfairly. These laws were called **'MIJ WCRO'** laws. The laws **ATEDSEGGRE** black and white people which meant the races were kept apart. In 1896 the **REMESUP OURTC** decided that these laws did not break the US **TIONCONTITSU**. The phrase **'ARATESEP** but **QUALE'** was used by the Supreme Court to sum up what it felt about segregation.

Activity 2

Wordsearch

Get a copy or make your own larger version of the wordbox shown here.

Use the wordsearch grid to hide five main words, names or ideas linked in some way with the Civil War. Complete the grid with random letters to conceal your words. Do not show where the words are on your grid. Your partner must find them. So, what you do is write definitions of the words below or beside your wordsearch.

When you have completed your wordsearch puzzle, exchange with your partner. Read their clues and find the word. As they solve your puzzle, you solve theirs.

Activity 3

The challenge! How far can you go?

The following questions go up in level of difficulty in pairs. The first two are easy. The last two are hard. How many will you try to do?

1 List three ways that black Americans were treated unfairly after 1865.
2 How did the Supreme Court make life harder for black Americans after 1896?

3 Why is the old vending machine (on page 30) an example of segregation of races in the USA?
4 How would you summarise the attitudes of many white people in the South towards black Americans?

5 What information would you use to support the view that black Americans were treated unfairly after 1865?
6 Give arguments for and against the Supreme Court decision of 1896.

Question practice

National 4

Source A is about the effect of the 'Jim Crow' laws written by an old black farmer in 1920.

SOURCE A

I remember my granddaddy telling me how he felt he was 'free at last' after the Civil War. 'Free at last boy', he said, 'thanks to these northern laws' – but it was all a lie. He died a few years ago. He knew he had been fooled. Jim Crow broke his spirit.

Source B is from a diary kept by a white woman in the South in 1920.

SOURCE B

My grandmother told me that freeing the slaves was the ruination of the South. Our plantations lost money and worst of all nigra folks [black people] walked the streets as if they were the equals of white folks. Something had to be done – I thank the Lord for good old Jim Crow.

Compare the views in Sources A and B about how people felt about the Jim Crow laws. Describe in detail their similarities and/or differences. You can also briefly compare the overall attitude of the sources.

Success criteria

▶ Examine the two sources in order to show two simple points of comparison or one developed point of similarity or difference.
▶ A simple comparison such as: 'Source A says... and Source B says ...' will get 1 mark.
▶ A developed comparison such as: 'Sources A and B disagree about how people felt about the "Jim Crow" laws. Source A says ... and Source B says ...' will get 2 marks.

National 5

Source A was written in 1890 by a woman who had grown up in the South after the US Civil War.

SOURCE A

My grandmother told me that freeing the slaves was the ruination of the South. Our plantations lost money and worst of all nigra folks [black people] walked the streets as if they were the equals of white folks. Something had to be done – I thank the Lord for good old Jim Crow. Jim Crow kept the nigras in their place. I had nothing against these folks who had been my mama's slaves but they were just not as good as us white folks.

Evaluate the usefulness of Source A as evidence about attitudes towards the Jim Crow laws in the late nineteenth century. **(5 marks)**

'Evaluate' means to judge a source as evidence for finding out about something. In this type of question it is never enough just to describe what is in a source. You must make your decision and give reasons to support your decision. It might be helpful to ask yourself *who* produced the source. Is that relevant in assessing the value of a source? *When* was the source produced and how might that help in the evaluation of the source? In this case it was just before the time of the Supreme Court decision.

You could start your answer like this but remember to write your reasons where you see the dots:

Source A is partly useful as evidence about attitudes towards Jim Crow because it was written by ... and this makes it useful because ... The source was written in 1890 and this makes it useful because ... .

Now keep going in that style. *Why* was the source produced? What did the person who produced the source want to achieve? Read the question again carefully. *What* information is in the source and how relevant is that to the question? What important information is missing from the source if you wanted a fuller picture of attitudes towards 'Jim Crow' laws?

Chapter 5 The attitudes and activities of the Ku Klux Klan

What is this chapter about?

The Ku Klux Klan (KKK) began in the 1860s as a way of using fear to control the newly freed black population in the South. By the 1870s the KKK had faded away, only to reappear in 1915. The new KKK claimed that immigrants, Catholics and Jews were threats to the American way of life. The KKK got away with most of the crimes it committed because many people in the police, the legal system and the courts were also members of the KKK or at least supported its ideas.

By the end of this chapter you should be able to:

▶ Describe some of the things done by the KKK to keep black Americans afraid.
▶ Explain why KKK members got away with so many crimes.

> Why was it so hard to fight back against the KKK?

How important was the Ku Klux Klan in preventing progress towards civil rights?

The Ku Klux Klan (KKK) started in the late 1860s as a way of controlling newly freed slaves through fear. The KKK terrorised rural communities with night-time raids on black households carried out by heavily armed men in scary disguises, as this picture on the right shows.

Rumours were deliberately put about that the KKK was really the returning ghosts of soldiers killed in the Civil War. The KKK spread quickly, supported by white southerners who wanted some way of controlling the large numbers of freed slaves. There were other violent racist groups in the South after the Civil War and as this poster shows, all these groups combined to make the lives of the newly freed slaves 'worse than slavery'.

How did the KKK become such an important influence by 1918?

The KKK was, and still is, a secret terrorist organisation which started in the southern states following the US Civil War. It died down in the late nineteenth century but in 1915 a new Klan was established, helped by a newly released blockbuster film called ***The Birth of a Nation***. The movie showed the KKK as protectors of southern white society against black terror. It was a huge success, becoming the first film to make over $10 million, and was the first movie to be shown in the White House, the home of the US president.

The image of the KKK in the film as heroic defenders of an American way of life was nonsense but many white Americans believed it. Black Americans knew that the KKK was an organisation that used fear and violence as ways of denying black Americans their civil rights.

A drawing of Klansmen in the 1870s.

GLOSSARY

The Birth of a Nation an influential film released in 1915

> What do the words mean? Why do the black couple look so distressed? Try to think of a least five reasons just by looking at the words and images in the picture.

'Worse than slavery.' If you cannot see the words on the picture clearly, search for it on the internet and find a larger version.

This was one of the first big films that rewrote history so that people believed the story in the film rather than the facts.

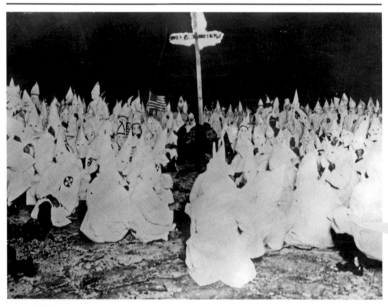

A photograph from the 1920s, 50 years after the 'worse than slavery' drawing was made.

> If the black couple in the previous drawing were alive, why would they still be distressed?

How was the KKK organised and what did it believe in?

The KKK was known as the **Invisible Empire** led by a **Grand Wizard of the Empire**. Local Klan organisations were called klaverns and KKK members had to be native-born Americans, white, Protestant, male and aged over 16 years. No black Americans, Roman Catholics or Jews were allowed to be in the KKK. There were special Klan sections for women.

By 1915 the KKK uniform had been created. Klansmen wore robes or sheets and masks topped with pointed hoods. The Klan's 'holy book', apart from the Bible, was called the Kloran!

GLOSSARY

Invisible Empire the official title of the Ku Klux Klan

Grand Wizard of the Empire the title of the Ku Klux Klan leader

The new KKK claimed to be a **patriotic** organisation protecting the 'American way of life' and devoted to '100 per cent Americanism'. The KKK attacked any group it called 'un-American'. That meant any group of people which the Klan believed was threatening traditional American life. In the 1920s, all non-Protestants, new immigrants and black Americans became targets for Klan attacks. The KKK used fear to stop black Americans registering to vote. It did not accept black people as equal citizens. In the South, the Klan's main targets were black Americans. An old farm worker remembered:

If coloured [black] folks tried to better themselves, the Ku Klux Klan would come and murder them. When voting time came round the Ku Klux would be waiting outside the voting place. No coloured folks would try to vote.

The Klansmen believed that black Americans were inferior human beings and were therefore against any civil rights laws. The Klan was also against Catholics, Jews and even divorced women. Until 1918 the KKK had little influence, but after 1920 it grew quickly.

The KKK burned large crosses on hillsides and near the homes of people they wished to frighten. If the intended victims still would not do what the Klansmen wanted them to do, victims might be kidnapped, whipped, mutilated or murdered. Masked Klansmen marched through the streets of towns and cities carrying posters threatening various people with punishment and warning others to leave town.

GLOSSARY

Patriotic loving or supporting your country

Lynching the illegal murder of someone, usually by a mob and usually for a racial reason

Federal national government of the USA

What was lynching?

Black Americans in the southern states lived in fear of **lynching**. Lynching meant black people being murdered by a mob who believed the black person had done something wrong. Victims were hanged and mutilated and their bodies sometimes burnt. The **federal** government did almost nothing to stop lynching and it was very difficult for black Americans to find justice in the South. The KKK was heavily involved in lynching.

In 1920, a newspaper reported a lynching:

The Negro was chained to the tree stump, beaten and then castrated. The fire was lit and a hundred men and women, young and old, joined hands and danced around the burning Negro. That night a big party was held in a nearby barn.

The point about a lynching is that it was illegal. There was no trial, no defence and no judge. Yet little was done to stop lynching. It was not until 1952 that no lynchings were reported – the very first year since the Civil War almost 90 years before. Of course, that does not necessarily mean that nobody was lynched.

Why is this such a shocking picture? Should such a picture be used in a school textbook about the struggle for civil rights in the USA?

Look carefully at the expressions on the faces of the all-white crowd watching a lynching.

What conclusions can you reach about the KKK from looking closely at this photo?

A photo of a Klan march through Washington, DC, the US capital city. In the background is the Capitol building, the heart of the US government.

How important was the KKK?

It is difficult to know how many members the Klan had because it was a secret organisation. One estimate of KKK membership, made in 1924, when the Klan was at the peak of its strength, was as high as three million people. The other point to remember is that the Klan did have important friends. In the 1920s, the KKK was powerful enough to hold large marches through Washington, the capital city of the USA.

It seemed as if nothing could be done to stop the terror tactics of the Klan. Although the KKK was popular with some Americans, the organisation was still illegal. It used terrorist tactics but few Klansmen were arrested and in some places the KKK was helped by local officials. By the end of the 1930s, the Klan was not as important as it had been, but terror, fear and the difficulty of winning any justice or fair treatment still dominated the minds of black Americans, especially in the South.

The novel *To Kill a Mockingbird* was published in 1960. The author, Harper Lee, based her story on events in her hometown in 1936 when she was 10 years old. The novel is set in Alabama in the **Deep South**. A lawyer, Atticus Finch, is appointed to defend Tom Robinson, a black man who has been accused of raping a young white woman. Finch becomes a figure of hate in the town for defending a black man. A white mob calls him a 'nigger-lover' when Finch helps to stop a mob from lynching Tom. Atticus Finch proves that Tom did not commit the crime but nevertheless the jury finds Tom guilty. Faced with the death penalty, Tom tries to escape from prison but is shot dead.

> **GLOSSARY**
> **Deep South** states in the USA which are the furthest from the North, such as Alabama and Georgia

The novel shows the intolerance, prejudice and race hatred that existed in the southern states of the USA in the 1930s.

Activity 1

Summarise this chapter

The following summary reminds you of what this chapter has been about. Words that are important in this chapter have been made into ANAGRAMS. Your task is to sort out the anagrams then write the correct version of this summary into your workbook or work file.

The Ku Klux Klan controlled the black population of the South with **ORTERR**. *The Klan was led by a* **RANDG ZIWARD** *and claimed to be protecting the* **RICANAMER YAW FO FELI**. *The Klan was involved in many* **INGSLYNCH**. *These were murders of black people who were thought by the KKK to have committed a crime.*

Activity 2

If this is the answer what is the question?

Below you will find a list of words or names. You have to make up a question that can only be answered by the word on the list. For example, if the word 'Crow' was the answer, a question could be 'What word follows Jim to describe laws that discriminated against black Americans?'

- Ku Klux Klan
- lynching
- The Birth of a Nation
- terror
- 1915
- 100 per cent Americanism
- klaverns.

Activity 3

This task is about both the 'Jim Crow' laws and the Ku Klux Klan. This can be an individual activity or done in small groups or pairs. The aim is to test each other's knowledge by making up a quiz.

▶ Your teacher will give you three Post-it® notes: one red, one orange and one green.
▶ You should make up three questions about the KKK or 'Jim Crow' laws in a time period allocated by your teacher. One should be easy (green), one tricky (orange) and one difficult (red). Questions should be put on the front and answers on the back.
▶ Put your initials in the bottom corner of each Post-it so everyone knows who made up the questions.
▶ When you are finished, put your Post-its up on the board.

▶ Your teacher will divide you into teams.
▶ Each member of the team should take it in turns to answer a question.
▶ Each correct answer gets a point. Incorrect answers get a point for the person who made up the question. Red questions should get most points, followed by orange and then green.
▶ Each team must try to answer at least one red, one orange and one green question.
▶ The team with the most points wins.

Activity 4

How did white society in the South try to control the black population?

This is a group activity and should be done in small groups or pairs. You will be asked to play a game called 'Just A Minute'. Your group must nominate a member of your team to talk about a topic given to you by your teacher. Suggested topics are listed below. You can add your own topics if you wish.

▶ the 'Jim Crow' laws
▶ the Ku Klux Klan
▶ *To Kill a Mockingbird*
▶ separate but equal
▶ lynching

You must talk for a whole minute, without hesitation or repeating yourself. If you get to the end of the minute without breaking the rules, you will get points.

Other teams can challenge you if they think you have broken the rules. If their challenge is judged to be correct, they will get a point and then can take over the remaining time. If their challenge is not correct, you will get a point and get to carry on speaking. The team with the most points wins.

Question practice

National 4

Source A is by John Kerr.

SOURCE A

The point to remember is that the Klan did have important friends. Few Klansmen were arrested and in some communities the Klan was helped by local officials. Each time the Klan came on a raid they were led by police cars.

Describe in your own words why the writer thought so little was done to stop lynchings by the Ku Klux Klan. You should use Source A and your own knowledge.

Success criteria

Make at least two factual points of information, or one developed piece of information, about why so little was done to stop the Ku Klux Klan.

National 5

Explain why it was so difficult for black Americans to gain civil rights before 1939. (5 marks)

In an 'explain' question you need to make five separate points from recall to gain all the marks. In the exam, you will get no help but there is some help here to get you started writing your answer. You will need to develop and explain your points with examples to get all the marks. You could write about:

▶ 'Jim Crow' laws
▶ fear of the Ku Klux Klan
▶ the results of the Supreme Court decision of 1896
▶ prejudiced and racist attitudes.

Chapter 6 Escape to the North?

What is this chapter about?

During the 1920s and 1930s there seemed little chance of life improving for black Americans in the southern states of the USA. 'Jim Crow' laws and the Ku Klux Klan combined to make life difficult and dangerous for black Americans, especially for any who had ambitions to improve their lives. During the First World War, many southern black Americans were attracted northwards by the offers of comparatively well-paid jobs in northern factories. The move northwards in search of a better life continued in the 1920s and 1930s.

By the end of this chapter you should be able to:

▶ Explain the factors that encouraged black Americans to move from the South to the North.
▶ Describe what life was like for many black Americans in the North.

What was the Great Migration?

Towards the end of the nineteenth century, black Americans began moving from their homes in the rural South to northern industrial cities. These migrants looked for better wages and a better life away from segregation and fear. The **Great Migration** increased dramatically in the years between 1910 and the early 1920s. About 500,000 black Americans moved to the North in this period, mainly because there were many unskilled factory jobs available during the First World War.

> ### GLOSSARY
> **Great Migration** the movement of black Americans from the South to northern cities around the First World War
>
> **Ghettos** areas of cities that had bad housing. They attracted black Americans because this housing was cheap

Was life better for black Americans in the northern cities?

The northern cities were known as the Promised Land. In the Bible, the Promised Land was a place where people would be safe and no longer slaves. Most of the black southern population was strongly Christian. They knew what the Promised Land was – and that it lay northwards.

When black Americans arrived from the South they were often poor. They looked for cheap housing and this tended to be in rundown areas. These poor areas became known as black **ghettos**. There was no official segregation in the North but in the northern cities the races were segregated by the area in which they lived.

The Great Migration of black Americans to the North may have made some problems worse. Competition for housing and jobs between white and black workers showed that segregation and discrimination existed in the North as well as the South. Black ghettos developed.

Why did race riots break out in the northern cities?

Race riots were often linked to racial tension growing in the northern cities. Competition between black and white Americans over jobs and housing strained relationships between the different racial groups in the cities. The riots usually started as small arguments between individuals but then spread quickly. The police, who were generally all white, usually sided with the white rioters. Federal troops often had to be brought in to restore order.

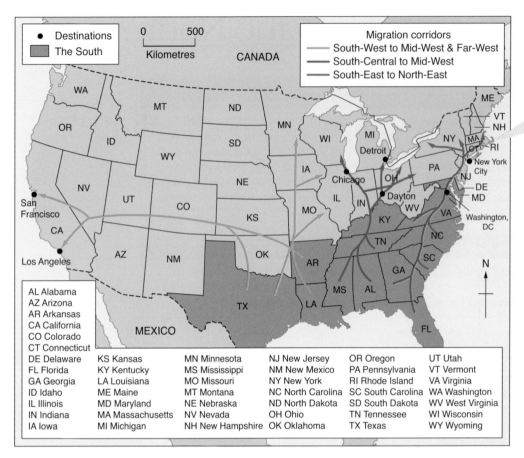

Describe in as much detail as you can what the map tells us about the Great Migration.

A map of the USA.

How do the people look? What might they be thinking? Do you think reality will match their expectations?

A family moving from Florida to New Jersey in 1940.

Think about the information that you have read in this chapter so far. Look at the pictures of the families. Would they still think the journey to the North had been worth it?

This family had just arrived in Chicago. By 1920, just over 50 per cent of Chicago's black American population was migrant.

The East St Louis riot in 1917 is an example of a small dispute that blew up into a riot. Two white police detectives were shot by black youths. In retaliation, a white mob invaded the black area of the town. Black women and children were beaten and a number of black men were lynched while the police watched. This riot left 50 people dead.

The Chicago riot of 1919 started when several black youths used a 'whites only' beach near Chicago. A row broke out and one black youth was hit by a stone and drowned. The police refused to arrest the white man accused by the black youths of throwing the stone. The black youths then attacked the police. That evening gangs of white teenagers began to set upon black Americans in Chicago. The city erupted into a five-day race riot that ended with 38 deaths, 537 serious injuries and large-scale destruction.

During the Second World War a riot in Detroit resulted in 34 deaths, hundreds of injuries and whole areas destroyed.

The riots showed that race problems did not only belong in the South. Federal politicians had to accept the fact that prejudice, discrimination and segregation existed in the North as well as in the South.

The cartoon tries to explain why many black Americans moved north.

How were black Americans helped by the move north?

The Great Migration opened up a brighter future for many black Americans and in the long run might have helped to force the federal government to do something about the race problem.

In the Harlem area of New York, the growth of black culture, music and art in the 1920s and 1930s was called the Harlem Renaissance (renaissance means rebirth). New black music, art and dance created a sense of pride in being black. Jazz music grew out of this sense of identity and many people say that jazz is the root of all of today's popular music such as rock, pop, hip-hop or rap.

Migration northwards continued steadily through the 1920s and 1930s but the 1940s saw the largest black migration from the South. During the Second World War, just like in the First World War, factories in the North needed as many workers as they could get. Once again, thousands of black people migrated northwards. In the 1940s, nearly one million black Americans made the move from South to North. By 1950, for the first time, a third of all black Americans lived outside the South. By the 1960s, over six million southern black people had migrated from the South to the North.

The experience of black Americans in the northern cities was to have a huge effect on the civil rights movement of the 1960s.

Activity

Summarise this chapter

Imagine that you are a journalist and that you have been asked to investigate and report on the Great Migration. Think about what sort of questions you might want to have answered. To help get you started, use the following:

▶ Why did so many black Americans move to northern cities?
▶ How were black Americans treated in the North?
▶ On balance, do you think black Americans who moved believed they had done the right thing?

Now follow these steps:

▶ Write the starter questions in your workbook or work file. Add your own questions.
▶ Find information and evidence to answer these questions.
▶ Note your answers in your workbook or work file.
▶ Now you can plan your article.
▶ Make notes and structure what you are going to write in your report.
▶ Write your first draft of your article.
▶ Find suitable illustrations for your article.
▶ Edit your article by making changes that you think are necessary.
▶ Check it with your teacher.
▶ When your teacher is happy, write your final version.

Success criteria

▶ You add at least one question to those provided.
▶ Information that answers all questions is found in the article.
▶ The article is well structured and well organised.

Question practice

National 4

Source A is from William Mahoney, a black American who moved north.

SOURCE A

I was sick and tired of being cheated and living in fear of my life. We never got a fair deal when we sold our cotton crop. If we complained the Klan came to visit us. There was no chance of changing anything.

Explain in your own words why so many black Americans travelled to the North. You should use Source A and your own knowledge.

Success criteria

Write at least two pieces of information explaining why so many black Americans travelled to the North.

National 5

Describe the problems that faced black Americans who moved north in the 1920s and 1930s. **(5 marks)**

- You must make a number of relevant, factual points.
- You will get 1 mark for each accurate, relevant key point of knowledge.
- You can get full marks by providing five straightforward points, by making three developed points, or a combination of these.

Chapter 7 The demand for civil rights after 1945

What is this chapter about?

Over a million black Americans fought for their country in the Second World War. They fought against Nazi aggression and racism, yet they faced segregation and racism in their own army units and back home in the USA. As a result, many black soldiers began to talk of the Double-V campaign. The 'V' stood for victory in the war and victory for civil rights back home in the USA. However, little happened to change things until 1954. In that year the Supreme Court overturned the 'separate but equal' decision of 1896. It showed that segregation was no longer acceptable in education and this opened the door to demands that segregation should end everywhere.

By the end of this chapter you should be able to:

▶ Describe the importance to the civil rights movement of the Double-V campaign, the *Brown* v. *Topeka* case and the murder of Emmett Till.
▶ Explain why the civil rights movement grew quickly after the Second World War and into the early 1950s.

Why did demands for civil rights grow after 1945?

The answer to this question can be summed up in three headings:
▶ The effect of the Second World War.
▶ The effect of the Supreme Court decision of 1954.
▶ The anger and motivation caused by the murder of Emmet Till.

Why was the Second World War important in leading to demands for greater civil rights?

Historians agree that the Second World War planted the seeds that grew into the civil rights movement of the 1950s and 1960s. Much of the credit for sowing those seeds should go to a man called A. Philip Randolph.

What did A. Philip Randolph achieve?

During the black migration to the northern cities in the early twentieth century, the porters were an important link between the North and South. The porters' job was to look after passengers who travelled on long-distance overnight trains. Since their work took them across the country, porters could carry news between black communities in the rural South and those in northern cities. The president of the Brotherhood of Sleeping Car Porters, a mainly black trade union, was A. Philip Randolph.

During the Second World World, A. Philip Randolph threatened a mass protest march in Washington unless **discrimination** in defence industry jobs and in the armed forces was ended. In 1941, Randolph and other black leaders met President Roosevelt. Randolph gave him a list of complaints about the lack of civil rights for black Americans. Randolph also made three demands:

> **GLOSSARY**
> **Discrimination** unfair treatment

▶ An immediate end to segregation and discrimination in federal government jobs.
▶ An end to segregation of the armed forces.
▶ Government support for an end to discrimination and segregation in all jobs in the USA.

President Roosevelt tried to convince Randolph that change must come slowly but Randolph and the other black leaders would not back down. Millions of jobs were being created in preparation for war (the USA did not join the Second World War until December 1941). Because of widespread discrimination, however, very few black Americans were getting any of the new jobs. Randolph said he was prepared to organise a march on Washington and bring 'ten, twenty, fifty thousand Negroes on the White House lawn' if their demands were not met.

President Roosevelt had been trying to drum up US support for a war against Hitler. One part of Roosevelt's campaign was to explain that the USA had to take action against Hitler to stop his racist policy against Jews and other minorities in Europe. Roosevelt also needed black soldiers to fight in the US armed forces. But, how could Roosevelt continue to claim the USA was fighting to get rid of racism when Randolph threatened to bring US racism into the spotlight of publicity? A march on Washington would be very embarrassing to the president since it would remind the world of the racism that existed in the USA.

Eventually, Roosevelt decided to give Randolph some of what he wanted and issued Executive Order 8802. The order stated that there would be no discrimination in the employment of workers in defence industries and in government on the basis of race, colour or religious beliefs. Roosevelt also established the Fair Employment Practices Committee to investigate any claims of unfair discrimination.

The second and third of Randolph's demands were not met. Segregation in the armed forces continued well into the 1950s while there seemed to be no chance of Randolph's third demand for an end to segregation in all jobs happening.

What was the Double-V campaign and how important was it?

When black American soldiers returned home from the Second World War they found that racism still existed. They wanted a change. They wanted civil rights. They said, 'No more Jim Crow'.

Even today, most people have no idea of the valuable contribution made by black American soldiers to the defeat of Hitler. Most films **airbrush** them out of history. More than half a million black American soldiers served in Europe. In 1941, pressure from A. Philip Randolph and others convinced the government to set up all-black combat units as experiments. They were designed to see if black American soldiers could perform military tasks on the same level as white soldiers.

> **GLOSSARY**
>
> **Airbrush** a way of making something vanish from sight in a photograph

The Tuskegee Airmen was the first group of black pilots ever trained by the US air force. They flew missions between 1944 and 1945, defending US bombers from German fighter planes. In 200 missions they never lost a bomber to enemy fire.

In one sense, the Double-V campaign failed; racial tensions continued during the war. As more and more people crowded into towns that had lots of factories making weapons, competition for housing and jobs resulted in race riots. In Detroit, 25 black and nine white people were killed before federal troops restored law and order. In 1943 in Harlem, New York, five black people died in riots. In the South there were also outbreaks of violent protest. There were up to 75 lynchings reported during the war.

A group photo of some of the Tuskegee Airmen.

On the other hand, the Double-V campaign sowed the seeds for later success.

The first small seed planted during the Second World War was the creation in 1942 of an organisation called the Congress of Racial Equality (CORE). This organisation was the beginning of a mass movement for civil rights. You will find out that the organisation played a big part in the civil rights protests of the 1950s and 1960s.

The second seed was an organisation called the Nation of Islam. Some black Americans refused to serve in the US armed forces. They believed in complete separation of the races and did not think it was right that black soldiers should fight for white USA. Their demands for separation were picked up later by Malcolm X and the Nation of Islam. You'll read about the Nation of Islam later in this book.

Protests and organisations that started before or during the Second World War eventually led to the more organised civil rights movement of the 1950s and 1960s. As one black American soldier said, 'After the end of the war, we just kept on fighting. It's just that simple.'

Why was the decision of the Supreme Court in 1954 so important to civil rights?

One of the first sparks to ignite the civil rights movement in the 1950s was an argument in a town called **Topeka** in the state of Kansas. The argument was about which school an eight-year-old girl called Linda Brown should go to. Oliver Brown, Linda's father, thought it was wrong that his daughter should have to go to a school for black children that was further away from her home and was less well looked after than nearby schools for white children.

In 1952, Mr Brown took the Topeka Board of Education to court over which school his daughter Linda could attend. Mr Brown was supported in this action by the National Association for the Advancement of Coloured People (NAACP). The NAACP aimed to achieve civil rights by working within the legal system. The NAACP saw the case of Linda Brown as an opportunity to attack segregation in education.

The court case was called 'Brown versus the Topeka Board of Education' (*Brown* v. *Topeka*) and eventually reached the Supreme Court. You should remember that in 1896 the Supreme Court had decided that segregation was acceptable. The Supreme Court said that black people and white people should have 'separate but equal' facilities, which included schools.

On 17 May 1954, the Supreme Court completely changed the decision reached nearly 60 years earlier. It decided that segregated schools were unequal and that schools should be desegregated. The court declared, 'in the field of public education the doctrine of "separate but equal" has no place'. In other words, the Supreme Court said the idea of 'separate but equal' had no place in modern-day USA and that separating children in schools because of the colour of their skin was wrong.

A woman sitting on the steps of the Supreme Court and holding a newspaper explains to her daughter the meaning of the Supreme Court's decision banning school segregation.

The court's decision was very important for the civil rights movement of the 1950s. The case of *Brown* v. *Topeka* and the Supreme Court decision was the first victory for civil rights campaigners. However, there was a long way to go. The problem now was how to make southern states desegregate their schools.

Even the US president, when he heard about the decision of the Supreme Court, said, 'I don't believe you can change the hearts of men with a law.' By the end of 1956 not one black child attended a white school in the South. Most southern states believed the Supreme Court was out of touch with the realities of southern life.

The realities of southern life were given national publicity with the third reason for the growth of civil rights after 1945: the murder of Emmett Till.

Who was Emmett Till and what happened to him?

In August 1955, a 14-year-old boy called Emmett Till went to visit relatives near Money, Mississippi. Emmett Till was from Chicago. He did not know about the severe segregation and prejudices that existed in Mississippi.

Emmett was a strong, well-built boy and looked like an adult. One of Emmett's friends told him there was a young white woman working in a local shop. They dared Emmett to speak to her. No one knows exactly what happened next but the white woman, Carolyn Bryant, the wife of the shopkeeper, said Emmet had used 'unprintable language' to her in the shop.

Kidnapped and murdered!

A few days later, two men drove up to the house of Emmett's uncle in the middle of the night. One of the men was Roy Bryant, the husband of the woman Emmett had spoken to. The two men grabbed Emmett and drove away with him. Three days later, Emmett Till's body was found in the Tallahatchie River. One eye was gouged out, and his crushed-in head had a bullet in it. There was a heavy engine tied round his neck with barbed wire. The corpse was nearly unrecognisable. The only way that Emmett could be recognised was by an initialled ring that he wore.

Bryant and his friend were arrested for kidnapping even before Emmett's body was found. Newspapers reported that all 'decent' people were disgusted with the murder and said that 'justice would be done'.

There they are!

The Emmett Till case quickly attracted national attention. Mamie Bradley, Emmett's mother, asked for her son's body to be taken back to Chicago. When it arrived, she was not sure the body was her son because it had been so beaten up. Emmett's mother was sickened but also angry. She insisted that her son lay in an open coffin so that local people and newspaper photographers could see what had happened to him.

Over four days, thousands of people saw Emmett's body. Pictures that appeared in magazines shocked many more people across the country. Black Americans from all across the USA were demanding that 'something be done in Mississippi now'.

The two men went on trial in a segregated courthouse in Sumner, Mississippi on 19 September 1955. The jury was entirely made up of white men and at that time in Mississippi, it was unheard of for a black man to accuse a white man of committing a crime. Nevertheless, Emmett's 64-year-old uncle was asked if he could point out the men who had kidnapped Emmett. Uncle Mose had been told he would be killed if he spoke up but he stood, pointed to Milam and Bryant, and said 'There they are.'

> From today's viewpoint, did Emmett's mother do the right thing in showing her son in an open coffin? Would your answer be different if you were black or white or lived in the North or South in 1955?

Over four days, thousands of people saw Emmett's body. Pictures that appeared in magazines shocked many more people across the country. All across the USA, black Americans were demanding that 'something be done in Mississippi now'.

Not guilty!

The all-white jury considered the evidence for just over an hour, and then gave a 'not guilty' verdict. The jury foreman later explained, 'I feel the state failed to prove that the body really was that of Emmett Till.' A few weeks later the two men found not guilty told their story to a newspaper and described how they really had murdered Emmett Till. At that time the **double jeopardy** law stated that a person could not be tried for the same crime twice. The men were safe even though they were murderers who sold their story for a profit.

> **GLOSSARY**
>
> **Double jeopardy** a law which states that a person cannot be put on trial for the same crime more than once

The importance of Emmett Till's death

The Emmett Till case had a big effect on the civil rights movement. The murder of a black person in the South was nothing new but what made it news was the publicity the trial got from new national media developments. Television was spreading across the USA and national news reporting of the murder and trial shocked the nation.

The North became aware of the full horror of segregation and persecution of black Americans in the South. In the words of Mamie Bradley (Emmett's mother), 'Two months ago I had a nice apartment in Chicago. I had a good job. I had a son. When something happened to the Negroes in the South I said, "That's their business, not mine … but not now".' Black Americans, in the North as well as in the South, would not easily forget the murder of Emmett Till.

Black American men who had served in the Second World War still remembered the Double-V campaign. The Supreme Court decision of 1954 showed that segregation could be changed. The murder of Emmett Till motivated people to push harder against the opening door of civil rights.

Activity 1

Summarise this chapter

The following summary reminds you of what this chapter has been about. Words that are important in this chapter have been made into ANAGRAMS. Your task is to sort out the anagrams then write the correct version of this summary into your workbook or work file.

During the war, many black troops began to speak of the **UDOBLE-V** campaign which stood for **TORYVIC** against the Nazis and **ISMRAC** in the USA. A big change happened in **5419** when the **REMESUP OURTC** decided that **SEGATIONREG** was no longer acceptable in schools. In the same year the murder of **MMETTE LLIT** shocked the US nation.

Activity 2

The challenge! How far can you go?

The following questions go up in level of difficulty in pairs. The first two are easy. The last two are hard. How many will you try to do?

1 Who or what was the Double-V campaign?
2 How did the *Brown* v. *Topeka* case lead to changes in civil rights?
3 Why did the Supreme Court decision of 1954 eventually lead to the end of the 'Jim Crow' laws?
4 Using what you now know, explain why the Supreme Court decision of 1954 was so important.
5 What conclusions can you make about the fears and worries of many white southerners following the Supreme Court decision of 1954?
6 Design a basic flowchart showing the growth of the civil rights movement between 1940 and 1954. Your chart should show the main events and main people involved in the campaign. Do your own research to find out more than is in this chapter – but keep it relevant to the years in focus!

Activity 3

Teach a lesson

In groups of three or four, your task is to teach a short lesson to the rest of your class which is linked to the theme of the growth of civil rights from the Second World War onwards. You must deal with the following core points:

▶ How did the war change attitudes among many black Americans?
▶ In what way did the *Brown* v. *Topeka* case lead to the weakening of 'Jim Crow' laws?
▶ Why did the NAACP think the *Brown* v. *Topeka* case could be useful to them?
▶ Why did the Emmett Till trial become such an important event in the growth of the civil rights campaign?

As in any lesson there are really important things for you, as the teacher, to decide on and to aim for:

▶ What do you want your students to be able to do and know at the end of your lesson?
▶ How will you assess the success of your lesson? In other words, what will you expect to see or hear from your students to prove that your lesson has been successful?

Your lesson should be presented in an organised, interesting, mature and informative way. Your main resource for information is this textbook but you must also do your own research, find, beg or borrow other resources to make your lesson come alive. Think of the times you have been bored just listening to someone talk. Your lesson must be different!

Planning is vital, and everyone in your group must participate. It would be helpful to assign tasks such as a gopher to fetch things, a timekeeper to watch how your time is being used, a facilitator to keep things running smoothly in your group (tact and diplomacy needed here!) and a recorder to note ideas before you all forget.

Negotiate the length of your lesson with your teacher. About five minutes would be appropriate. It must have visual material; PowerPoint is just one of the possibilities.

Question practice

National 4

Source A is from *The Eyes on the Prize*, a book by Juan Williams about the civil rights campaign.

SOURCE A

> *By the time the war ended in 1945 it was clear that nothing at home would ever be quite the same again where the black struggle for freedom and justice was concerned.*

Explain why the Second World War caused important changes in black people's attitudes to civil rights.

You should use Source A and your own knowledge.

Success criteria

Write at least two pieces of information explaining how the Second World War caused important changes in black people's attitudes to civil rights.

National 5

Explain why the civil rights movement grew in the years following the Second World War. **(5 marks)**

To be successful in this type of question you must give five reasons why something happened. In your answer, you must use accurate and detailed information from your own knowledge.

There will be no source to help you in the exam but here are some words and prompts to jog your memory and help you write your answer.

- Double-V campaign.
- *Brown* v. *Topeka*.
- Supreme Court decision of 1954.
- The trial of the murderers of Emmet Till.
- The importance of national television news reporting.

Chapter 8 The Montgomery Bus Boycott and Martin Luther King Jr

What is this chapter about?

The bus boycott in Montgomery, Alabama was one of the first successful protests in the campaign for civil rights and had important results for the movement. On its own, the bus boycott did not achieve very much. It did not end all segregation and Montgomery remained a segregated town. On the other hand, the bus boycott showed what could be achieved by organised, peaceful and non-violent protest. An important result of the boycott was the emergence of a new civil rights leader: Martin Luther King Jr.

By the end of this chapter you should be able to:

▶ Describe how the Montgomery Bus Boycott started.
▶ Explain why the Montgomery Bus Boycott was important to the civil rights movement.

How did the Montgomery Bus Boycott begin?

On a December night in 1955 in the city of Montgomery, Alabama, Rosa Parks was going home after a long day working in a large city-centre shop. She sat in the black section of the bus. When the white people's section of the bus was full and more white people got on, the driver moved the sign marking the boundary between white and black seats to create more white seats. Rosa Parks was now sitting in the white area. The driver asked her to move. She refused. The driver had her arrested.

At first there was no bus **boycott**. Rosa Parks was a member of the **NAACP** and the NAACP had been waiting for just such an opportunity to launch a high-profile campaign against segregation in the city buses. There had been lots of times when black youths had been arrested for challenging bus segregation but the youths were unlikely to be reliable in a court of law. Rosa Parks was a mature woman and a respected person among her black and white colleagues in the shop where she worked.

Remember the date: it was 1955. This was just one year after the US Supreme Court had declared that segregation was wrong in schools. The NAACP wanted to argue that if segregation was wrong in schools, was it not also wrong in everyday life, such as on buses?

Suddenly, the focus shifted away from the NAACP plans. When news spread of the arrest of Rosa Parks, 50 respected leaders of the black community met in a Montgomery church to

> **GLOSSARY**
> **Boycott** to deliberately stop doing something to create pressure for change
> **NAACP** National Association for the Advancement of Coloured People – a civil rights organisation

Rosa Parks photographed at the time of her arrest on 1 December 1955.

discuss their plans. They agreed to boycott the city bus system. In the group was a young Baptist minister in his first job at that church: Martin Luther King Jr.

Why was a boycott started?

One year before the arrest of Rosa Parks, a letter written to the mayor of Montgomery had explained why it was in the bus company's interests to end segregation.

Seventy per cent of the riders on the buses are Negroes. If the Negroes did not use the buses, then the bus company could not operate. More and more of our people are already arranging with neighbours and friends to keep from being insulted and humiliated by bus drivers. Plans are being made to ride less, or not at all, on your buses.

The mayor refused to stop segregation on buses, which meant that black passengers still had to pay their fare at the front door but could only take a seat in the black section after they walked to the back door of the bus to get on. The black community argued they were humiliated each time they used a bus.

Eventually, the Supreme Court decided that segregation on Montgomery's buses was against the US constitution. The buses were officially desegregated in December 1956 after a boycott that lasted for 381 days. However, the bus company had started to desegregate anyway. The company could not afford to lose black passengers.

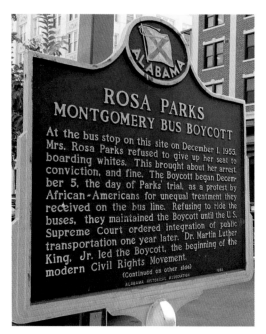

A plaque commemorates the site in Montgomery, Alabama where Rosa Parks was arrested.

Why was the Montgomery Bus Boycott important?

- The protest showed what could be achieved by people if they stayed united and determined to achieve their target. For months, black Americans refused to use the buses in Montgomery.
- The boycott also showed how effective peaceful, non-violent protest could be. The police found it difficult to cope with a **civil rights** protest that was organised, broke no law and was peaceful. How could they arrest people who simply did not get on buses?
- The boycott showed the economic power of the black community. Since black Americans made up 60–70 per cent of all bus passengers, the bus company was faced with a choice: desegregate its buses or go out of business. For the first time the black population had shown its economic power.
- Finally, the bus boycott introduced Martin Luther King Jr to the civil rights protest. He was to become one of the most famous black leaders of the twentieth century.

> **GLOSSARY**
>
> **Civil rights** everyone in a country should be treated the same

Who was Martin Luther King Jr?

Martin Luther King Jr was born on 15 January 1929 in Atlanta, Georgia. His father was a church minister who also was called Martin. That is why Martin Luther King Jr has 'Jr' for junior after his name.

When he was a boy growing up in Atlanta, King experienced segregation and discrimination for himself. In 1953, King married Coretta Scott and, in 1954, was given his first job as pastor at the Dexter Avenue Baptist Church in Montgomery, Alabama. He was still only 25 years old. King and his wife had been in Montgomery for less than a year when the bus boycott began.

King tried to help people to understand why Rosa Parks and others felt they had to make a stand against segregation. He declared:

there comes a time when people get tired – tired of being segregated and humiliated: tired of being kicked about by the brutal feet of oppression.

King was a good-looking man in his thirties and presented a non-threatening image of black protest to the US television audience. Most importantly, he was an inspirational speaker and leader who was prepared to be arrested, criticised and even put his own life at risk for the cause he believed in: civil rights.

King worked with another church minister called Ralph Abernathy to organise the year-long Montgomery Bus Boycott. The bus boycott success made King into a well-known national leader of the civil rights movement.

What were the ideas of Martin Luther King Jr?

When King was growing up he was inspired by Mahatma Gandhi, who had used non-violent protest successfully against the British rulers of India in the 1940s. Gandhi had realised he would never win against the huge force of the British Empire by using violence. However, simply by disobeying laws that he believed to be unfair and dressing as a very poor man, Gandhi gained world attention and humiliated the British rulers when they used force to stop him.

Ghandi's actions were a major factor in India gaining independance from Britain in 1948. His campaign taught Martin Luther King Jr an important lesson for the future.

King believed that non-violent, peaceful **civil disobedience** was the best weapon in the fight for civil rights. King felt that if a law was wrong, then the citizens of the country had the right and the responsibility to protest about it. If he and his followers were arrested that was fine, because the prisons all across the South would be filled with civil rights protesters and that would give the campaign even more publicity. When King spoke to a

The pictures on pages 54–6 show some things linked to the Montgomery Bus Boycott but they are the usual sort of pictures you would expect to see. Using a search engine such as Google Images, find up to five better images to make the point about the bus boycott more effectively. Make clear why you have chosen your images.

Martin Luther King Jr stands in front of a bus at the end of the Montgomery Bus Boycott on 26 December 1956.

GLOSSARY
Civil disobedience deliberately refusing to obey laws

Mahatma Gandhi attending Indian independence talks at 10 Downing Street, London.

crowd of white racists outside a church in Alabama, he said he would not obey evil laws. He also said that he and his followers intended to wear down the resistance of white racists by using endless protests.

King also made it clear that he would not use violence. During the Montgomery Bus Boycott in December 1955 he said:

In our protest there will be no cross burnings. There will be no threats or bullying. No white person will be taken from his house by a hooded Negro mob and brutally murdered. Love your enemies and pray for them.

What was the SCLC?

In 1957, King, Reverend Ralph Abernathy and others formed the Southern Christian Leadership Conference (SCLC) to campaign for civil rights. When King was made SCLC president in 1960, he became more and more involved in the use of non-violent civil disobedience as a way of campaigning for civil rights.

In the early 1960s, King led many demonstrations in the South aimed at ending segregation and allowing black Americans to vote freely. In 1964, King became famous around the world when he made a speech which became known as the 'I Have a Dream' speech and *Time* magazine (an important national magazine in the USA) chose King as their 'Man of the Year'. This was the first time a black American had ever been given the title. Later, in 1964, King also won the Nobel Peace Prize. He was the youngest man ever to win it. He was still only 35 years old.

Activity 1

Chapter summary

The following summary reminds you of what this chapter has been about. Words that are important in this chapter have been made into ANAGRAMS. Your task is to sort out the anagrams then write the correct version of this summary into your workbook or work file.

In 1955 a **SUB COTTBOY** started in **GOMERYMONT, BAMAAAL**. It began when **AROS KSPAR** refused to give up her **TSEA** on a **SUB**. The **TTBOYCO** grew into a challenge against **ATIONSEGREG** and led to more **LIVCI IGHTSR** protests. The **TTBOYCO** showed the **NOMICECO** power of the black community. The boycott was important because it led to the rise of **TINMAR THERLU INGK RJ** as a leader of the civil right movement. King believed in **IVILC EDIENCEDISOB**.

Activity 2

If this is the answer what is the question?

Below you will find a list of words or names. You have to make up a question that can only be answered by the word or words on the list. For example, if the world 'Montgomery' was the answer, a question could be 'where did the bus boycott happen in 1955?'

- Rosa Parks
- 70 per cent
- Martin Luther King Jr
- boycott
- NAACP
- 381
- December 1956
- Gandhi
- non-violent protest.

Question practice

National 4

Source A is from a speech by Martin Luther King Jr on 5 December 1955.

SOURCE A

We are here because of the bus situation in Montgomery. We are here because we are determined to get the situation corrected.

Describe the main causes and events of the Montgomery Bus Boycott.

Success criteria

Write at least two factual points of information, or one developed piece of information, about the Montgomery Bus Boycott.

National 5

Your task now is to write an 'explain' question about the Montgomery Bus Boycott. 'Explain' questions often start like this: 'Explain the reasons why … .' To be successful in answering this type of question you must give five or six reasons why something happened, so your question must allow someone to make that same number of points in the answer.

You will be able to check that you have allowed for a wide-enough question when you write your own mark scheme. That means you must list the points you would expect to see in a good answer. This question is worth 5 or 6 marks so you must include at least five or six points in your mark scheme.

When you have completed this task, exchange your work with a partner and you answer their question while they answer yours. After ten minutes stop writing, give your work to your partner who wrote the mark scheme and she or he will mark your work while you mark their answer.

Chapter 9 Little Rock

What is this chapter about?

Many southern states attempted to ignore the US Supreme Court's 1954 decision to end segregation in schools. In 1957, a protest organised by the NAACP at Little Rock High School, Arkansas, led to a situation that became worldwide news. The world asked why it was necessary for armed US soldiers to escort teenage students to and from their school.

By the end of this chapter you should be able to:

▶ Describe what happened at Little Rock High School in 1957.
▶ Explain why the world was shocked by what happened to Elizabeth Eckford.

What happened at Little Rock High School in the state of Arkansas in 1957?

Although the US Supreme Court's decision of 1954 had outlawed school segregation, southern states tried to ignore this ruling. Schools in the South which did try to desegregate were met by furious white racist mobs. The mobs, along with Ku Klux Klan (KKK) members, attacked black students. Schools were even blown up. The most famous struggle to integrate schools was in Little Rock, the capital city of **Arkansas**.

In September 1957, the NAACP decided it would test the willingness of states in the South to desegregate their schools. Little Rock High School was a very successful all-white school. In 1955, the school board had agreed to start integration in the autumn of 1957. The NAACP selected nine grade A students so that the school could have no complaints about the ability of the new black students.

The news of this attempted integration ripped through the white parts of Little Rock. It was clear from what was said by white racists in the city that black students trying to go to Little Rock High School would be risking their lives. Even the KKK promised to take action.

The NAACP knew there was a huge danger to the nine black students due to go to school, so the students were telephoned and told *not* to attend the next day. The problem was that one student, Elizabeth Eckford, did not have a phone so she was not warned to stay at home. The next day she turned up at school, on her own, to face a white mob. Elizabeth also had to face a line of soldiers blocking her path.

The governor of Arkansas, **Orval Faubus**, had ordered a line of troops from the **National Guard** to block the

GLOSSARY

Arkansas a state in the South – Little Rock is its capital city

Orval Faubus the Arkansas state governor in 1957

National Guard a state-controlled military force made up of part-time members

Gloria Ray Terrance Roberts Melba Patillo

Elizabeth Eckford Ernest Green MinniJean Brown

Jefferson Thomas Carlotta Walls Thelma Mothershed

'The Little Rock Nine.'

path to the school. These soldiers were part of the Arkansas National Guard and looked just like regular US army soldiers.

Faubus argued that he had used the National Guard to keep the mob away from the black students. In effect, what the National Guard did was to form a human blockade, preventing the black students getting to the school.

This is how Elizabeth Eckford remembers her attempts to get to school:

My knees stared to shake and I wondered if I would make it to school. The crowd moved closer and closer. Somebody started yelling 'Drag her over to this tree! Let's take care of that nigger.' I tried to see a friendly face somewhere in the crowd – someone who maybe could help. I looked into the face of an old woman and it seemed a kind face, but when I looked at her again, she spat on me.

White students of Little Rock High School shout insults at Elizabeth Eckford (wearing sunglasses).

The sight of National Guardsmen and screaming white crowds stopping an American child going to school made national news headlines. Soon afterwards the events at Little Rock became world news.

Why did events at Little Rock become a national and international issue?

By the mid-1950s, most US homes had television sets. For the first time, people could see what was happening in places such as Little Rock. The world was shocked when it saw and heard what happened to a 15-year-old girl trying to go to school.

The late 1950s were also the time of the Cold War. This was a war of words and propaganda between the USA, which claimed it was the home of freedom, and Communist Russia, which was described as the Red Enemy. (Remember the Red Scare of 1920 discussed on page 19? It was happening all over again in 1950s' USA.)

When film of Elizabeth Eckford being bullied and threatened just for attending a white school was shown round the world, Russia used those images to claim that the USA was very far from being a land of the free. President **Dwight Eisenhower** was embarrassed. Something had to be done.

> **GLOSSARY**
>
> **Dwight Eisenhower** President of the USA in 1957

What did the president do to solve the crisis?

The US president was no longer willing to have individual states in the USA ignoring federal law. Nor was he prepared to allow the USA to be criticised in the world's newspapers. When Faubus removed the National Guardsmen, there was now nothing to stop the mob from attacking any black student going to school in Little Rock. President Eisenhower took action. He sent 1000 US paratroopers to 'invade' Arkansas. These soldiers would then protect black children on their way to school.

Armed soldiers carrying rifles with fixed bayonets surrounded the black students on their way to school. When they travelled to and from school, the students were protected by troops in jeeps with machine guns.

The soldiers stayed in Little Rock for a year and they even patrolled the school corridors to make sure the children were safe. Naturally, the events in Little Rock attracted worldwide attention to the civil rights movement.

Eventually, the tension died down as the interest of the media went elsewhere but the black students in Little Rock were still bullied. Ernest Green was the first black student to graduate from Little Rock High School in 1958 but it took a long time to solve the issue of school integration.

In 1962, a black student, James Meredith, attempted to attend the University of Mississippi Law School. His admission was blocked, and during the violence that followed, federal troops were once again used to restore order and enforce national law.

Black students being protected by armed soldiers.

The Mississippi authorities tried to ban Meredith from the university because he was black. However, the federal government decided that Meredith should be allowed into the law school. On Sunday 30 September 1962, 123 federal marshals, 316 US border patrolmen, and 97 federal prison guards escorted Meredith to the college campus. Facing Meredith and his protectors was a mob of over 2000 men and women. Riots broke out and two journalists were killed.

President Kennedy had to send 16,000 troops to protect Meredith and restore order at the university. Twenty-eight US marshals had been shot and another 160 of the law enforcers were injured. Federal troops remained at the university for over a year just to protect one black student.

James Meredith (centre) being escorted to university by US federal marshals.

Did the Civil Rights Act of 1957 make much of a difference?

After the events in Montgomery, Alabama and Little Rock, Arkansas, the US government introduced the Civil Rights Act in 1957. The Civil Rights Act was not a huge step, but it was the first national act on civil rights for nearly 100 years. Opinion was divided as to the importance of the act. On one hand, it seemed to show that the federal government was no longer willing to allow the southern states to do as they pleased as far as race relations were concerned. On the other hand, some civil rights campaigners were disappointed with the limited power of the act. By 1959 the new Civil Rights Act had not added a single southern black person's name to the voting register. The pressure for civil rights continued to grow during the early 1960s.

Activity 1

Chapter summary

The following summary reminds you of what this chapter has been about. Words that are important in this chapter have been made into ANAGRAMS. Your task is to sort out the anagrams then write the correct version of this summary into your workbook or work file.

The **REMESUP OURTC** had stated that **ATIONSEGREG** in schools was wrong. In 1957 the **NAACP** decided to find out what had changed by sending nine black schoolchildren to **ITTLEL OCKR** High School. On the first day, only **BETHELIZA FORDECK** turned up and she was met by an **GRYAN BOM**. Eventually, **US DIERSSOL** were used to keep the black children safe at school.

Activity 2

Draw a storyboard of at least six frames telling the story of the events at Little Rock High School in 1957. Each frame should have words that make clear what that part of the story is about.

You must include:

▶ Elizabeth Eckford going to school
▶ the National Guard blocking Elizabeth Eckford's path
▶ an angry white crowd threatening Elizabeth Eckford
▶ US troops protecting the black students
▶ black students finally graduating from Little Rock High School.

Success criteria

Your storyboard must be attractive and interesting. It must tell the story of Little Rock in 1957 so that even a stranger would know what your story is about.

Question practice

National 4

Source A was said by a young black soldier in 1957.

SOURCE A

When I heard what the Supreme Court said about segregation in schools being wrong I hoped things would change. Three years later when I saw US soldiers helping black kids get to school in the South, then I KNEW things were changing.

Explain in your own words why the US soldier was so excited. You should use Source A and your own knowledge.

Success criteria

Write an answer with at least two pieces of information explaining the effect of sending black students to Little Rock High School in 1957.

National 5

Source A was said by a white student at Little Rock in 1957.

SOURCE A

The moment they walk in we will walk out. They have schools just as good as ours. They should stay in their own schools. They will just bring down the standards here. Black kids just can't mix with white students. It ain't right.

Source B is from an interview with an NAACP member at Little Rock, 1957.

SOURCE B

The Supreme Court decision of 1954 was clear – separate but equal just does not work. Why should grade A black students be denied the same standards as white students? The Little Rock Nine have been chosen because of the excellent grades. They are a credit to any High School. Segregation must end NOW!

Compare the opinions in Sources A and B about the integration of Little Rock High School. **(4 marks)**

This is a 'comparison' question. 'Comparison' questions are easy to spot because they are the only ones that will refer to two sources.

A comparison question asks you to make clear connections between sources. The skill being assessed is your ability to *compare* and that does not mean your ability to describe two sources. So you will not get marks for simply writing 'Source A says …' and then 'Source B says …'. By all means do that as part of your answer but you should also explain the point you are making by using your own words. That is what is meant by a developed comparison. Finally, you need to show three simple comparison points between the sources or you could explain one comparison fully and then do one other shorter comparison. For example, you could start by writing something like this:

The sources disagree about the integration of Little Rock High School. Source A shows that white students thought that integration 'ain't right' but the writer of Source B says that 'segregation must end NOW!'

What you have done so far is make the point that you know the sources disagree and you have provided evidence from each source to back up your point. Now, write three more paragraphs, each one explaining a way in which the sources disagree and then using quotations from the sources to back up your point.

The second paragraph has been started for you:

The sources disagree about the ability of the Little Rock Nine. Source A states … while Source B disagrees by saying, … .

Chapter 10 Sit-ins and Freedom Rides

What is this chapter about?

The years 1960 and 1961 were a time of big change in the civil rights movement. In those years a new, younger and more instant form of protest was born. Two such protest methods were sit-ins and Freedom Rides. The actions of black and white students put new life into the civil rights movement. Sit-ins and Freedom Rides challenged segregation in the South and pushed the federal government into taking action to enforce federal law and change southern racist attitudes.

By the end of this chapter you should be able to:

▶ Describe what happened at sit-ins and on the Freedom Rides.
▶ Explain why student groups started sit-ins and went on Freedom Rides.

What were sit-ins?

The **sit-ins** were part of an **SNCC** campaign for civil rights. Black students had created the SNCC in April 1960 to help co-ordinate, support and publicise the sit-in campaign. SNCC stood for Student Non-violent Co-ordinating Committee and its first targets were segregated lunch counters across the South.

Lunch counters were like fast-food cafés with a counter where food was served. At the counter, there were stools for white customers only. When a mixture of white and black SNCC students sat down at lunch counters, it marked the beginning of 'sit-ins', an effective method of using civil disobedience in peaceful protest.

> **GLOSSARY**
>
> **Sit-in** a non-violent protest of blocking an area by remaining seated
>
> **SNCC** Student Non-violent Co-ordinating Committee, a civil rights group

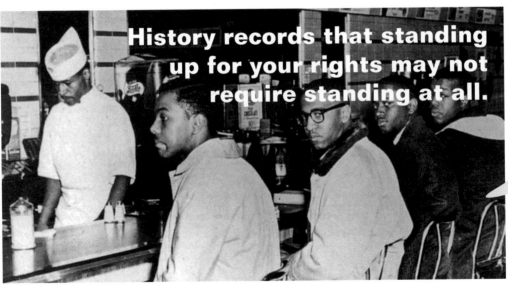

History records that standing up for your rights may not require standing at all.

> Can you explain why the words have been added to this picture? How has the word 'standing' been used in different ways to make the point?

A photograph of black protestors at a sit-in.

The students of the SNCC were well organised and well prepared. Protest classes were run by a student called Jim Lawson in the University of Nashville. In Lawson's classes, students prepared for the day they would have to remain non-violent even when they were being assaulted and insulted.

On 1 February 1960, four black students sat down and attempted to order some food at a whites-only lunch counter in Greensboro, North Carolina. They were refused service but remained in their seats until closing time. They returned the following day with 25 supporters who continued the sit-in. By 5 February there were more than 300 students, black and white, taking part in the protest.

Television news showed local white youths attacking the demonstrators but when the police arrived it was the demonstrators who were arrested. However, as soon as the demonstrators were carried away from the lunch counters, more demonstrators took their place. The police, the prisons and the courts all over the South were being overwhelmed by the campaign to 'fill the jails'.

By the end of the year, more than 700,000 protestors had participated in sit-ins across the country. Although thousands of the students were arrested and physically assaulted, they refused to retaliate. The campaign methods of the students are a good example of civil disobedience and non-violent protest.

> Describe exactly what you see happening. How does this illustrate the protest methods used by the civil rights movement around 1960?

A sit-in taking place in the 1960s.

How successful were the sit-ins?

In many ways, the sit-ins were highly successful. National television coverage highlighted the violent racist reaction of many southerners, while the courage, commitment and sacrifice of the demonstrators won them support across the USA. By the summer of 1960, many lunch counters in the South had been desegregated. However, the sit-ins did not end all segregation in the South and their impact was only really felt at a local level.

What were the Freedom Rides?

In 1960, a Supreme Court decision had banned segregation in public areas such as toilets, waiting rooms and restaurants for bus travellers going from one state to another.

In 1961, a group of black and white members of a non-violent protest group called the Congress of Racial Equality (CORE) wanted to see if such segregation really had ended.

In May 1961, 13 CORE members travelled from Washington, DC to New Orleans in the southern state of Mississippi. The bus journeys were called **Freedom Rides** and the passengers became known as Freedom Riders. Along with CORE members there were SNCC members.

> **GLOSSARY**
> **Freedom Rides** travelling on buses to check and challenge racial segregation

The plan was to travel south on **interstate** buses. Interstate highways (like motorways) and the service area toilets were the responsibility of the national federal authority, not the state authority. In areas under federal authority there should have been no segregation. The Freedom Riders wanted to see if segregation in interstate public facilities had really ended. Black students would try to use whites-only toilets and white students would use black-only toilets at stopping points along the route.

This is what one white student called William Mahoney found at the first stopping point on his journey:

At our first stop in Virginia I saw what a southern white called 'separate but equal'. A modern rest station with gleaming counters was labelled 'white' and a small wooden shack beside it was tagged 'coloured'. The coloured waiting room was filthy and in need of repair and overcrowded.

The Freedom Riders expected a violent reaction from the southern racists. At first, there was little violence, but as they travelled south, bus tyres were slashed, buses were firebombed and the Freedom Riders were beaten up.

The Freedom Riders were met with heavy resistance from southern whites who knew the route that the students were following. When the buses arrived in Alabama, the Ku Klux Klan was waiting for them. In Anniston, Alabama, two 'Freedom' buses were stopped and burned. Passengers who tried to get off were beaten. The students then travelled to Birmingham, Alabama, where they got on to another interstate bus. The bus was again stopped and eight white men boarded the bus. They brutally beat the students with sticks and chains. One of the students, James Peck, had to have 50 stitches in his head. Even when faced by such vicious attacks, the students stuck to their non-violent protest beliefs.

Did the Freedom Rides help to gain civil rights?

The intention of CORE was to gain publicity for its protest and it achieved this aim. Once again, the television news coverage of the attacks on the Freedom Riders deeply shocked the American public. Martin Luther King Jr attempted to persuade the riders to stop for fear that they would be killed, but the Freedom Rides continued throughout the summer – as did the violence.

Freedom Riders on a bus in Washington, DC.

Search on YouTube for the 'Freedom Riders movie'.

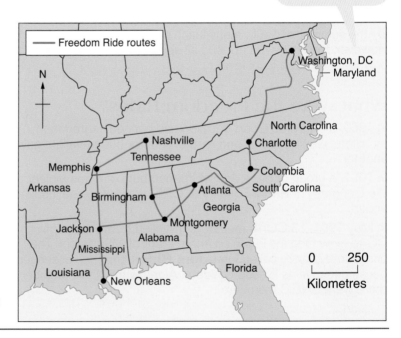

A map showing the routes of the Freedom Rides.

Another aim of the protestors was to force the federal government in Washington to take action.

President Kennedy was concerned about the Freedom Rides and he sent one of his advisers to see first hand what was happening. When the president's adviser arrived, he was beaten unconscious. Eventually police escorts were provided for the riders, although this did not prevent further violence.

The **FBI** was then asked to investigate the violence used against the students and US law officers were also sent in to protect the students. As the risk of serious violence increased, Martin Luther King Jr once again attempted to get the students to stop, but they refused. CORE and SNCC agreed to continue the bus rides.

GLOSSARY

FBI Federal Bureau of Investigation, the US federal detective agency

Eventually, in the face of national publicity and pressure to change, new orders were sent to all interstate bus companies that ended segregation at interstate bus stations. Finally, in late 1961, the US government ordered the end of segregation in airports, rail and bus stations.

How important were the Freedom Rides?

The Freedom Riders, like the sit-ins before them, were successful in making northern white Americans more and more sympathetic towards the civil rights cause. Many people agree that of all the tactics used, the Freedom Riders did the most to increase support for the civil rights movement.

A CORE publicity leaflet said:

The Freedom Rides, like the sit-ins before them, demonstrated that anyone who opposed segregation could take action themselves to work towards ending Jim Crow laws. They helped the spread of civil rights through the south.

However, there are different opinions about how important the Freedom Rides were. There is a view that the Freedom Rides did not do much to change the real problem which was that black Americans had little power to alter the way the country was run. As Jim Lawson, writing in the *Southern Patriot* newspaper, reported in 1961:

The Freedom Rides won concessions but not real changes. Police help keep the peace and let us use interstate restrooms but there will be no revolution until we see Negro faces in powerful positions in this country.

Activity 1

Read this chapter about sit-ins and Freedom Rides carefully. Which of the following statements do you think are correct?

Copy out the statements that you think are correct. You should be able to explain why the other statements are incorrect.

- CORE organised sit-ins.
- CORE stood for the Council of Racial Equality.
- Sit-ins were to stop segregation in the USA.
- Sit-ins were attempts by white people to stop black Americans from using lunch counters.
- Sit-ins were supported by many people in the South.
- Sit-ins were attempts by black people to sit at lunch counters and challenge segregation laws.
- The SNCC was a civil rights organisation that took part in sit-ins and Freedom Rides.

- SNCC stood for Student Campaigns Co-ordinated Committee.
- Protestors aimed to 'fill the jails' and bring the legal system to a halt.
- Sit-ins were successful.
- Sit-ins were partially successful.
- Freedom Rides were not successful.
- Freedom Rides were extremely dangerous to the protestors.
- Freedom Rides were partially successful.

Activity 2

Work in pairs. In this activity make up at least five questions which you would use to test someone's understanding of the sit-ins and the Freedom Rides. To make up the questions, first work out what you want to ask. You must have a clear idea of what answer you want for each question so avoid questions that are vague and have no focus such as 'What do you think about the sit-ins?' A good question would be 'What effect did the Freedom Rides have on public opinion in the USA?'

Avoid questions that ask 'who was …' or 'when was …'. Also, don't ask questions that have one-word answers: they are not allowed! Your questions should be mature, well presented and test real understanding. The purpose is to help learning, not to catch people out with really tricky questions.

When you have both completed five questions, try them out on each other. Can your partner answer your question? And can you answer your partner's question in exchange?

The ones to remember are the questions you couldn't answer. They provide a guide to what you are less sure about and therefore a guide to revision.

Repeat this exercise either now or at a later date – and try it out on different topics.

Question practice

National 4

Source A was said by a Freedom Rider called William Mahoney.

SOURCE A

At our first stop in Virginia I saw what a southern white called 'separate but equal'. A modern rest station with gleaming counters was labelled 'White' and a small wooden shack beside it was tagged 'coloured'. The coloured waiting room was filthy and in need of repair and overcrowded.

Explain in your own words why the Freedom Riders travelled south. You should use Source A and your own knowledge.

Success criteria

Write at least two pieces of information explaining the purpose of the Freedom Rides.

National 5

Describe the results of the sit-ins and Freedom Rides. **(6 marks)**

In 'describe' questions you will be asked either to describe what happened or to describe the effects of something. That really means just tell a straightforward story with about five or six pieces of information. You do not need to say why anything happened. What you do need to do is include as much correct and relevant information as you can from your own memory. There will be no source to help you. And remember – answer the question that you are asked, not the one you would like to be asked.

Chapter 11 Birmingham, Alabama 1963

What is this chapter about?

By 1962 there was still no change on the big issue of civil rights for all black Americans in the USA. Martin Luther King Jr knew that something had to be done to force change. The place King chose to do something was Birmingham, Alabama and he knew that he faced the toughest fight of the civil rights campaign. As a result of the violence that erupted in Birmingham, President Kennedy was forced to take federal action.

By the end of this chapter you should be able to:

▶ Describe the events that shocked the world in Birmingham 1963.
▶ Explain why the events in Birmingham were useful to the civil rights movement.

Why was the civil rights movement facing problems in 1962?

It is easy for us to look back at an event in the past and know what happened next but the same is not true for people living at the time. You have no idea what will happen to you tonight, next week or in ten years' time. The point is that we can all be wise in **hindsight**. In early 1962 the civil rights demonstrations had only won small victories and made limited progress. King and the other leaders had no idea if the civil rights demonstrations would be successful or not.

A big demonstration involving Martin Luther King Jr and the SCLC in Albany had failed to achieve any real changes. Many civil rights protestors were disheartened.

The civil rights demonstrations also depended on large numbers of protestors who were prepared to break the law and risk going to prison. Usually, the SCLC would get its supporters out of prison by paying bail but after the demonstration in Albany the movement was losing money. Supporters were now afraid that if they stayed in prison they would lose their jobs and their families would suffer. As a result, King's reputation as a leader was weakened and he knew he had to grab the headlines back and achieve success. The place he chose to do that was Birmingham, Alabama.

> ### GLOSSARY
> **Hindsight** looking back on events and thinking you know better than the people at the time

> How might this image have been used in the early 1960s? You can find many violent images from Birmingham, Alabama in 1963 by searching the internet. This image is very different.

An old postcard from Birmingham, Alabama.

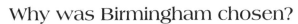

Why was Birmingham chosen?

Martin Luther King Jr described Birmingham as being the most segregated city in the USA and explained:

I think I should give the reason for my being in Birmingham. Birmingham is probably the most segregated city in the United States. Its ugly record of police brutality is known in every section of the country. There have been more unsolved bombings of Negro homes and churches in Birmingham than in any city in this nation. These are the hard, brutal and unbelievable facts.

King knew that civil rights protesters would be risking their lives when they arrived in Birmingham. The Ku Klux Klan (KKK) in Birmingham was one of the most violent in the entire USA. Klan members were responsible for dozens of bombings throughout the area. One of the civil rights leaders called the city 'Bombingham' because of the violence that was common there. It was also no secret that the Klan had the support of the Birmingham police force, led by Eugene 'Bull' Connor.

Added to this, George Wallace, the new governor of Alabama, was totally opposed to the civil rights movement. He famously proclaimed: 'Segregation now, segregation tomorrow, segregation forever.' It was make or break time for the civil rights movement.

The two main leaders of the demonstration in Birmingham were Martin Luther King Jr and the Reverend Fred Shuttlesworth. They had made clear their objectives: to desegregate public facilities and department stores. However, even those limited aims were too much for the Birmingham police.

Even before the march started, King and Shuttlesworth were arrested for planning to break an order not to march. While he was in prison, King wrote a reply to those who said that black Americans should wait for white America to give slow changes:

*I guess it is easy for those who have never felt segregation to say wait. But when you have seen vicious mobs lynch your fathers and mothers and drown your brothers and sisters … when your tongue becomes twisted as you try to explain to your six-year-old daughter why she can't go to the amusement park advertised on TV and see the tears welling up in her little eyes when you tell her that **Funtown** is closed to coloured children … then you will know why it is difficult to wait.*

> ## GLOSSARY
>
> **Funtown** a theme park that black children could not go to
>
> **Project C** the name of the protest campaign launched by the civil rights movement in Birmingham

What was Project C?

When King and Shuttlesworth were released from prison, a new campaign plan was made called **Project C**. The 'C' stood for confrontation. King knew the police chief in Birmingham, Eugene 'Bull' Connor, was a violent racist. He also knew that if he could provoke Connor into taking extreme action then the cameras would show images that would shock the world. At first, the demonstrations, boycotts and sit-ins achieved little. As the weeks dragged on, King then decided to use a very risky strategy. King's plan involved using Birmingham's black schoolchildren.

'WE'VE GOT A JOB'

Black schoolchildren demonstrating in Birmingham, 1963.

What do the words 'We've got a job' mean in the context of the photograph from Birmingham 1963? What caption would you write to this picture?

Why was the USA shocked by events in Birmingham?

King and other young black leaders realised the importance of television and the media. They hoped that images of white racist police attacking black schoolchildren would cause public opinion to swing behind the civil rights campaign and force the US government to take action.

On 2 May 1963, over 1000 schoolchildren marched through Birmingham – and Connor was waiting for them. Connor was determined not to give in to the civil rights demonstrators. As soon as the children began to march, he ordered the arrest of all of the students. Over 900 children from the ages of six to 18 were jailed. The following day, Connor called out the water cannons and the dogs. As marchers came parading down the streets, the police attacked. Connor used fire hoses, billy clubs (batons like baseball bats) and dogs to attack the peaceful protesters.

American people watched their televisions in shock and disbelief as white police officers savagely attacked schoolchildren first with powerful fire hoses and then with tear gas, dogs and even electric cattle prods.

This photo had the caption 'How a photograph rallied civil rights support.' What does the caption mean and do you agree with it?

Firefighters aim hoses at demonstrators in Birmingham in 1963.

Was Project C effective?

Martin Luther King Jr's tactics were risky but they worked. The world had been shocked by pictures of children being attacked by police dogs and washed down the streets by fire hoses in Birmingham. However, the SCLC was having second thoughts. King wanted to call the march off. He was concerned about the violence being suffered by the demonstrators. They were getting good publicity but at a terrible cost.

On the other side of the 'battle', local businessmen were desperate for a solution. Their trade had collapsed and the bad publicity that Birmingham was getting on national television was likely to damage their businesses for a long time. Even black Americans in Birmingham were against the tactics used by the civil rights campaigners. After the protests were over, the black Americans who lived in Birmingham still had to live with the hostility from the white Americans in the city.

Both black and white businessmen knew that the bad publicity was ruining the reputation of Birmingham for everyone so they got together to sort out a deal. They agreed that toilets, lunch counters, changing rooms and water fountains would be desegregated within 90 days.

When word leaked out about the deal, the local KKK was furious. Klansmen rioted in the city and firebombed several black churches, businesses and homes. An event in a local motel showed just how closely linked the Klan was to the local law officers. Many of the civil rights protesters were staying at the Gaston Motel which was firebombed by the KKK. As the occupants ran out of the building, they were attacked by Alabama state police. Several of the protesters were seriously injured, but this time they fought back. A riot broke out. When it was all over, 40 people had been injured and seven shops were destroyed by fire. Many black Americans were also wondering if non-violent peaceful protest really was the best policy.

Why did President Kennedy get involved?

President Kennedy was forced to take federal action. He realised that only federal action and federal law could stop the violence that had sparked off in Birmingham from spreading across the USA. Kennedy appeared on television and promised action on **racism** based on the principle that 'race has no place in American life or law'.

> **GLOSSARY**
>
> **Racism** treating people differently because of the colour of their skin

Public sympathy for civil rights was high and Kennedy could not ignore the mood of the public. Kennedy ordered an end to segregation in Birmingham. By 13 May, 3000 federal troops were on the streets of Birmingham to restore order.

Activity 1

If this is the answer what is the question?

Below you will find a list of words or names. You have to make up a question that can only be answered by the word on the list. For example, if the word 'Birmingham' was the answer, a question could be 'What was the name of the city that was called the most segregated in the USA?'

- Project C
- Albany
- Bull Connor
- 'Bombingham'
- George Wallace
- police dogs and fire hoses
- Fred Shuttlesworth
- Gaston Motel
- John F. Kennedy.

Activity 2

Design a revision mobile

The activity is to design a mobile to illustrate the tactics and methods of the civil rights movement between 1955 and 1962. You can choose to work on your own or as part of a group no larger than four. If you work in a group, you must also design and use a creativity log in which you record exactly what each person in the group contributed to the final mobile.

Success criteria

- Your mobile must have at least four strands.
- Each strand should be about a main event in the civil rights campaign.
- Each strand should have several mobile items attached.
- Each strand must have two text items, perhaps only one significant name or word.
- Each strand must have at least one large double-sided illustration linked to an event or personality.
- Each strand must have a three-dimensional feature that represents a major event in its strand.
- Your mobile should hang easily.
- Your mobile must be able to be read from a distance.
- Your mobile must be attractive, colourful and relevant to the project task.

Question practice

National 4

How successful were the civil rights protests between 1955 and 1962?

Use the historical information in this chapter and anything else you can discover to design an information poster. This information poster should show:

- the different protests made by the civil rights movement between 1955 and 1962
- how much the protests improved civil rights in the USA – or didn't.

There are a variety of ways you can design this. A few ideas are listed below.

- You may wish to divide your information poster into 'successes' and 'failures'.
- Or, you could present the information in the form of a leaflet, a mind-map or a storyboard that tells the story of civil rights protests between 1955 and 1962.
- There may also be an opportunity for you to design a slideshow presentation that can be shared with the class or saved on your school's website for revision.

You can produce your own images or you can print off images from the internet to cut out and stick on to your information poster to make a collage.

It is important to remember that you will only be assessed on your historical understanding and not on the artistic qualities of your information poster. However, it should be presented in a clear and neat manner to allow your audience to fully understand your main ideas.

National 5

To what extent did the civil rights protests of the 1950s and early 1960s make a real improvement to the lives of black Americans? (8 marks)

There is no source provided for a 'to what extent' question. You will only get one 'to what extent' question in your entire National 5 exam paper. To be successful in this type of question you need to decide how important something was in explaining why something happened. In this case, you are asked how important the civil rights protests were in improving the lives of black Americans.

You must come up with at least five points and organise them into a balanced answer. 'Balanced' means looking at the successes and failures and thinking about which was most important. You must then write a short conclusion that sums up your answer to the question.

Chapter 12 'I Have a Dream'

What is this chapter about?

A few months after the Project C demonstrations in Birmingham, Alabama, the civil rights movement united to plan a huge March on Washington. It was intended to keep up the pressure on US President Kennedy. During the March on Washington, Martin Luther King Jr delivered his 'I Have a Dream' speech which made clear to the world exactly why the civil rights movement existed. In 1964, it looked as if all the hopes of the civil rights movement had been realised when the US government passed the Civil Rights Act.

By the end of this chapter you should be able to:

▶ Describe how the events of Project C in Birmingham led eventually to the Civil Rights Act of 1964.
▶ Explain why support from President Kennedy and federal authority was so important to the civil rights movement.

Is there a link between the Birmingham campaign and the March on Washington in August 1963?

Yes, there is. First, Martin Luther King Jr's reputation increased hugely after the Birmingham campaign and most of the world saw him as the leader of the civil rights movement. Second, President **John F. Kennedy** had promised **federal authority** to give civil rights to all black Americans.

The protests of the early 1960s – sit-ins, the Freedom Rides and the Birmingham demonstrations – all increased the pressure on President Kennedy to do something about civil rights. On the evening of 11 June 1963, Kennedy spoke on national television to explain what he intended to do and why he intended to do it. He said:

The events at Birmingham have so increased the cries for equality that no nation can choose to ignore them. I am, therefore, asking the Congress to enact **legislation** *giving all Americans the right to be served in facilities which are open to the public. I am also asking* **Congress** *... to end segregation in public schools.*

> ### GLOSSARY
>
> **John F. Kennedy** president of the USA from 1960 until his assassination in 1963
>
> **Federal authority** the national government of the USA
>
> **Legislation** new laws
>
> **Congress** like the UK Parliament, it makes laws

How could pressure be kept on Kennedy to keep his promise?

Civil rights leaders knew it would not be easy to get a new civil rights law passed. Politicians, such as Governor Wallace of Alabama, had said they would stop it becoming law.

In the 1940s, A. Philip Randolph had suggested a March on Washington in an attempt to force the US government to improve civil rights. He had been persuaded not to organise the march by promises that civil rights would improve. However, 20 years later it looked as if nothing had been achieved. What could be done now to make sure that the federal government kept its promise? In the summer of 1963 the time seemed right to carry out a March for Jobs and Freedom.

While black leaders organised the march, politicians in Washington were afraid that there would be violence. Kennedy, however, saw it as an opportunity to gain support from black Americans.

How many adjectives (describing words) can you list that could be used in relation to this picture?

What was the purpose of the March on Washington?

On 28 August 1963, over 200,000 black and white people marched towards the **Lincoln Memorial** in Washington. The site was significant because President Lincoln had freed the slaves 100 years before.

The huge gathering of demonstrators was not designed to gain anything other than publicity, which it achieved brilliantly. It was the largest civil rights demonstration in US history and four national television channels broadcast the event live. The speech that Martin Luther King Jr gave has become known as the 'I Have a Dream' speech and is considered to be one of the most famous and important speeches of the twentieth century.

I have a dream that my four little children will one day live in a nation where they will not be judged by the colour of their skin but by the content of their character … I have a dream that even the state of Mississippi will one day be transformed into an oasis of freedom and justice. So let freedom ring out. When we allow freedom to ring from every town and every hamlet, from every state and every city we will be able to speed up that day when all God's children will be able to join hands and sing in the words of the old Negro song 'Free at last! Free at last! Great God Almighty, we are Free at last'.

Martin Luther King Jr, 'I Have a Dream' speech, 1963.

Crowds in Washington, DC in 1963.

GLOSSARY

Lincoln Memorial a monument to President Lincoln, who had been assassinated in 1865. He was the president who had ended slavery in the USA

Assassinated murdered for political reasons

King and other leaders of the civil rights movement felt that they had a friend in President Kennedy. By 1963, Kennedy seemed to support the movement wholeheartedly. However, in November 1963, Kennedy was **assassinated**.

The March on Washington had put the civil rights movement back in the headlines but when President Kennedy was assassinated it looked like the movement had gained nothing. However, the new president, called Lyndon B. Johnson, made sure that the Civil Rights Act became law.

Imagine you were a reporter in Washington in 1963. How would you accurately report the meaning and some of the content of King's speech?

Martin Luther King Jr delivering his speech. Read the full text of his speech (find it on the internet) and watch it on YouTube.

Years of protests eventually resulted in the 1964 Civil Rights Act. When the act was being discussed by the US government, all southern politicians fought against it with all their energy. However, it did become law, and was the most important new civil rights law at that time. It did a great deal to get rid of discrimination and segregation.

What did the Civil Rights Act of 1964 do?

The Civil Rights Act of 1964 made discrimination and segregation based on skin colour or race illegal. Discrimination on the basis of race in any or all public places in the USA was banned. This included petrol stations, restaurants, hotels, cinemas and airline terminals.

There were also to be equal opportunities in the workplace. It became unlawful for a business employing more than 25 people to discriminate on the basis of race, national origin, religion or gender. The federal Justice Department was allowed to prosecute any state government that still discriminated against black people.

How important was the Civil Rights Act of 1964?

Most people agreed that the Civil Rights Act was a big move towards helping black Americans achieve full civil rights. Of course, it was impossible to make a law to change the way that people thought and felt. However, many politicians believed the Civil Rights Act had gone as far as the law could to help black Americans.

On the other hand, some black Americans were concerned that the Civil Rights Act did nothing to solve discrimination in housing or give black people a fair and free vote. The act did not end fear and discrimination. The Ku Klux Klan, often helped by the police, still used terror against any black person who tried to use the freedoms that the act was supposed to guarantee.

Activity 1

Summarise this chapter

The following summary reminds you of what this chapter has been about. Words that are important in this chapter have been made into ANAGRAMS. Your task is to sort out the anagrams then write the correct version of this summary into your workbook or work file.

After the **P CTCROJE** demonstrations in **HAMBIRMING**, Alabama, the civil rights movement united to plan a huge **CHMAR** on **TONWASHING**. It was intended to keep pressure on President **NNEDYKE**. When the marchers gathered at the **COLNLIN ORIALMEM** in Washington, DC, Martin Luther King Jr gave a famous **EECHSP** known as the 'I Have a **MREAD**' speech in which he said that black Americans were almost **REEF TA SLAT**. In 1964 it looked as if all the hopes of the civil rights movement had been realises when the US government passed the **LIVIC IGHTSR TCA**.

Activity 2

The challenge! How far can you go?

The following questions go up in level of difficulty in pairs. The first two are easy. The last two are hard. How many will you try to do?

1 From the following list, choose the two best answers to this question: 'How important was the publicity gained from the Project C demonstration in Birmingham?':
  ▸ segregation was still a problem
  ▸ President Kennedy said he would help pass a law to give civil rights
  ▸ Martin Luther King Jr made a speech
  ▸ public opinion across the USA supported civil rights
  ▸ Project C achieved very little.
  What is the best answer?

2 Give reasons using some factual examples to support your choices in question 1.

3 Can you explain why the March on Washington was organised?
4 How would you summarise what Martin Luther King Jr meant when he said 'I Have a Dream'?

5 What would you say was the importance of the Civil Rights Act of 1964?
6 Suppose you could have advised Martin Luther King Jr from early 1962. Would you have suggested he do things differently? If yes, what would you have suggested and why? If no, why would you not have suggested he do anything differently?

Activity 3

This is a National 5 activity

In pairs, each of you make up one 'describe' question and one 'explain' question based on the information in this chapter. Remember that these types of question are worth 5 or 6 marks. You must also make up a mark scheme to help someone mark the answer. Remember to include at least five or six points in your mark scheme.

Now exchange your questions with another pair and answer their questions. After 10–12 minutes collect the answers to the questions you set. Mark the answers using your mark scheme. Give feedback to the person who answered your question. Feedback should be encouraging. Mention the good parts of the answer. Suggest ways that the answer could be improved.

Question practice

National 4

Source A is from a television broadcast made by President Kennedy in June 1963.

SOURCE A

The events at Birmingham have increased the cries for equality. It ought to be possible for every American to enjoy the privileges of being American without regard to his race or his colour.

Describe in your own words why President Kennedy decided to support a new civil rights law. You should use Source A and your own knowledge.

Success criteria

Write at least two factual points of information, or one developed piece of information, about why Kennedy decided to support a civil rights law.

National 5

Describe how it is possible to link the publicity gained from Project C directly to the Civil Rights Act of 1964. **(5 marks)**

This is a 'describe' question. In this type of question you will be asked to describe either what happened or the effects of an event or development. To be successful you need to include five or six pieces of detailed and accurate recall information. You must give as much detail as you can manage in eight or nine minutes. In the exam there will be no source to help you so your answer will be based on your own recall.

Top tip: answer the question. The question does not ask you to describe the events at Birmingham, Alabama in 1962. It is about what happened afterwards. Always answer the question that you are asked, *not* the one you would like to be asked.

Helpful clues: when planning your answer you could look at the immediate, short-term results such as public opinion and sympathy for the civil rights movement or you could look more widely at how Project C led to a change in federal support and the way the civil rights movement kept up pressure on the government until a new law was created.

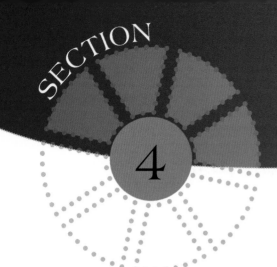

SECTION **4**

The ghettos and black American radicalism

Chapter 13 Voting rights in 1965

What is this chapter about?

The Civil Rights Act of 1964 was a big move towards helping black Americans achieve full civil rights. This chapter is about the campaign to make it easier for black Americans to vote. The campaign reached its peak in March 1965 when Martin Luther King Jr led a march from Selma to Montgomery, Alabama. The campaign leaders knew that the march would meet violent white resistance. Publicity had worked in Birmingham, so why not in Selma?

By the end of this chapter you should be able to:

▶ Describe the events of the Selma to Montgomery march.
▶ Explain why voter registration was so important and how the events at Edmund Pettus Bridge were so closely linked to the Voting Rights Act.

Why was it so difficult for black people to vote?

The Civil Rights Act of 1964 did not end fear and discrimination. The Ku Klux Klan still used terror against any black person who tried to use the freedoms that the act was supposed to guarantee. Martin Luther King Jr and others argued that the only way to get real change was to get rid of the racists in local and state politics. He said that the new Civil Rights Act gave black people 'some part of their rightful dignity, but without the vote it was dignity without strength'. King believed that the right to vote without fear or difficulty was vital if civil rights were to mean anything at all. Black Americans were still in the majority in many southern cities and could easily elect their own leaders into positions of power if only they had the opportunity to vote for them.

The problem was that very few black Americans had registered to vote. In the USA, any adult who wants to vote must first of all register. Black Americans had been given the right to vote in 1870, but in the years that followed white authorities who ran the **voter registration** offices in the southern states made it almost impossible for black Americans to register.

The civil rights movement now aimed to get more black Americans voting. That meant campaigners had to be able to do so without fear of violence or threats. It also meant that any unfair barriers that stopped black Americans voting would have to be removed.

> **GLOSSARY**
>
> **Voter registration** in the USA all people with the right to vote must register before they can cast their vote

Selma, Alabama, 1965.

Look at this picture carefully. Think what the picture shows and how it was used. What caption would you write to go with this picture?

In many areas of the South, 'Jim Crow' laws made it hard for black Americans to qualify for the vote. For white supporters of segregation, the consequences of allowing black Americans to vote were unthinkable. It would end white power in the South. Black politicians would be elected!

Why was Selma, Alabama chosen as the focus of protest?

Selma, Alabama had 15,000 black adults who should have had the right to vote, but only 335 had been able to register. That meant that only about one person out of 50 with the right to vote was actually able to vote. During 1963 and 1964, hundreds of black Americans who should have had the right to vote freely were prevented from voting by difficulties created when they tried to register at the courthouse in Selma.

In January and February 1965, protests were held in Selma to bring attention to the actions of the white racists who were denying black Americans their legal rights. Civil rights leaders, including Martin Luther King Jr, decided to hold a protest march from Selma to Montgomery on 7 March 1965.

Black leaders had learned that one of the main reasons why President Kennedy had become involved in the civil rights issue was because public opinion had been shocked by the violence used by white police during Project C.

The civil rights campaign leaders knew very well that a large march from Selma to Montgomery would be met by violent white resistance, especially since the governor of Alabama, George Wallace, had already promised 'Segregation forever!'. The **sheriff** of Selma, Jim Clark, was also known to be very like Eugene Connor, the police chief in Birmingham, Alabama, in his attitudes and the speed at which he lost his temper.

> **GLOSSARY**
> **Sheriff** the chief of the local police

On 1 February 1965, over a month before the march was due to take place, King got himself arrested quite deliberately. He had just gained fame as the winner of the Nobel Peace Prize, a world-famous award. He was on the front cover of almost every magazine and newspaper. He was on television news and chat shows almost every night.

King's arrest was therefore big news and it is now clear that this was a sort of publicity stunt. Before he was arrested, King and others in the SCLC had prepared a letter that would be sent to newspapers when King was in prison. On 5 February the *New York Times* printed the message:

Why are we in jail? When the Civil Rights Act of 1964 was passed many decent Americans thought the day of difficult struggle was over. By jailing hundreds of Negroes the city of Selma, Alabama has revealed the persisting ugliness of segregation. There are more Negroes in jail with me than there are on the voting registers. This is the USA in 1965. We are in jail because we cannot tolerate these conditions for our nation.

Sunday, 7 March 1965 was the starting date for the Selma to Montgomery march. Approximately 600 marchers started out. On the Edmund Pettus Bridge the marchers were met by about 200 state troopers and local police mounted on horseback. The police were all armed with tear gas, sticks and whips. The marchers were ordered to turn back. When they did not, the marchers were attacked by the law enforcement officers. The air filled with tear gas and marchers were beaten, whipped and trampled by the horses. Finally, they turned around and went back to Selma. Seventeen marchers were hospitalised.

The effect of television coverage of the march

Television coverage of the march and the attack caused national anger. Sunday 7 March 1965 – 'Bloody Sunday', as the day became known – was a turning point in the campaign for fair voting. All across the USA people were horrified at what they saw on television.

Eventually, Martin Luther King Jr and his supporters gained legal permission to march from Selma to Montgomery. On 21 March, the march began again. This time US troops protected the marchers. At the end of the Selma to Montgomery march on 25 March 1965, King spoke to the 25,000 marchers and once again made it clear what the purpose of the civil rights campaign was:

America's conscience has been sleeping but now it is waking up.

Let us march on segregated housing …

Let us march on segregated schools …

Let us march on poverty …

Let us march on ballot boxes …

Let us march on to the American Dream.

> Search YouTube for 'Selma campaign 1965' and watch what happened when this photo was being taken.

The aftermath of the Selma to Montgomery march in March 1965.

Was the Selma march successful?

Many people believe that Martin Luther King Jr and the other civil rights leaders not only expected violence from white authorities but even wanted it. The demonstrators knew that television news would turn public opinion against the white racists and they hoped that televised racist violence would persuade the government to do something about voter registration. If true, then their plan worked!

In August 1965, Congress passed the Voting Rights Act which removed various barriers to registration such as the ability to read and write. Literacy had often been

Discuss how this could be used as proof that the Selma to Montgomery march had been successful.

'I got one of 'em just as she almost made it back to the church.' A cartoon published in a US newspaper in 1965.

used to stop black Americans voting. President Johnson even made clear that he would sign the new law in the same room where, a century before, President Lincoln signed a document to free slaves who had been made to fight for the southern armies in the US Civil War.

The effect of the Voting Rights Act

By the end of 1965, over 250,000 black voters were newly registered. Within three years of the act being passed most of the black population of the South was registered to vote.

In Mississippi in 1960 there were 22,000 black Americans registered to vote; six years later there were 175,000. In Alabama in 1960 there were 66,000 black Americans registered to vote; six years later there were 250,000.

The 1965 act was a big move towards making voting rights a reality for thousands of black Americans in the South. The act said there were to be no more literacy tests or checks on **poll tax** payments which had been used to prevent black Americans from voting in the past. The new law also helped to improve the living and working conditions of many black Americans because white politicians now realised they needed black voters if they wanted to stay in power.

> **GLOSSARY**
>
> **Poll tax** a local tax, the payment of which was often used as evidence that people were entitled to vote

Many black Americans now saw an opportunity to become politicians themselves and in 2009 Barack Obama became the first black president of the USA.

The Voting Rights Act marked the end of the civil rights campaigns in the South. Segregation, discrimination and 'Jim Crow' laws had been outlawed, if not entirely removed. It is always easier to change laws than to change what people believe, no matter how wrong those beliefs might be.

By 1965 the focus of civil rights protests moved north and the style of protest also changed. Non-violence protest was about to become violent.

Activity 1

Wordsearch

Get a copy or make your own version of the wordbox shown here.

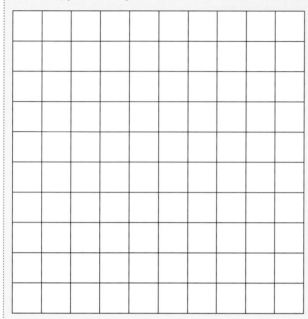

Use the wordsearch grid to hide five main words, names or ideas linked in some way with the campaign for voting rights. Complete the grid with random letters to conceal your words. Do not show where the words are on your grid. Your partner must find them. So, what you do is write definitions of the words below or beside your wordsearch.

When you have completed your wordsearch puzzle, exchange with your partner. Read their clues and find the word. As they solve your puzzle, you solve theirs.

Activity 2

Sketch a sketch!

Work in pairs. The aim is for each of you to draw part of a cartoon or sketch and see how long it takes for your partner to work out what your cartoon is about. When she or he has worked it out, complete your drawing and give it a title.

Activity 3

The challenge! How far can you go?

The following questions go up in level of difficulty in pairs. The first two are easy. The last two are hard. How many will you try to do?

1 Can you suggest another word or phrase for 'protest'?
2 Why did Martin Luther King Jr continue to campaign for voting rights after the Civil Rights Act was passed in 1964?

3 King said that the new Civil Rights Act gave black people 'some part of their rightful dignity, but without the vote it was dignity without strength'. How could you say that in your own words?
4 How would you summarise the attitude of Governor Wallace towards the civil rights movement?

5 What evidence could you suggest to support King's decision to challenge white authority by marching over the Edmund Pettus Bridge?
6 Do you agree that King's strategy to win a Voting Rights Act was successful, both in the short and long term? Give reasons for your answer.

Question practice

National 4

Source A is adapted from a newspaper report written by George B. Leonard in March 1965.

SOURCE A

There are moments when a nation is outraged and that outrage turns to action. One of these moments came when national television showed a group of Negroes at Selma who were gassed, clubbed and trampled by horses.

Describe in your own words what took place at the Edmund Pettus Bridge in March 1965, why it occurred and what happened as a result of what people saw on their televisions. You should use Source A and your own knowledge.

Success criteria

Include at least two factual points of information, or one developed piece of information, on the events and results of the march over the Edmund Pettus Bridge in March 1965.

National 5

This is a 'how useful' question so you must judge a source as evidence for finding out about something. In this type of question it is never enough just to describe what is in a source.

▶ It would be wise to base your answer around who produced the source. Is that important in assessing the value of a source?
▶ When was the source produced and how might that help in the evaluation of the source?
▶ Why was the source produced? What did the person who produced the source want to achieve?
▶ What information is in the source and how relevant is that to the question?
▶ What important information is missing from the source but would be relevant to answering a question about the campaign to gain voting rights?

Source A was written by a journalist called George B. Leonard who watched the events of 'Bloody Sunday' on television and described his own reaction.

SOURCE A

The chief purpose of the civil rights movement has been to awaken the nation's conscience. Hundreds of people dropped whatever they were doing, some would leave home without changing clothes, would borrow money, hitch-hike, board planes, buses and trains, travel thousands of miles with no luggage; all these people would move for a single purpose: to place themselves alongside the Negroes they had watched on television.

Evaluate the usefulness of Source A as evidence of the effects of television news reporting of the events at the Edmund Pettus Bridge in March 1965.
(6 marks)

Chapter 14 Black Radicals and Black Power

What is this chapter about?

By the middle of the 1960s, the civil rights movement had changed. Many young black Americans were disillusioned by the failure of the southern-based civil rights campaign to improve conditions in the cities of the North and West of the USA. Stokely Carmichael started to speak about 'Black Power' and both he and Malcolm X rejected white help.

In 1966, a new group – the Black Panthers – grabbed the headlines as one of the most radical protest groups. The new groups who used violent direct action in their protests were called collectively black radicals.

By the end of this chapter you should be able to:

▶ Describe the different black radical groups in 1960s' USA.

▶ Explain why black Americans in the cities were attracted to the black radical groups.

Why did the civil rights movement split in the 1960s?

From the mid-1960s onwards, disagreements increased about what the civil rights movement should do next. The movement had always contained different points of view about the use of violence. Those differences in opinion came to a head during the March Against Fear in 1966. During the march, the differences between the non-violent strategies of Martin Luther King Jr and the more militant campaigners became obvious. While King and his supporters chanted 'Freedom Now' and encouraged white Americans to join the march, the new leader of the SNCC called Stokely Carmichael chanted 'Black Power' and rejected white help.

Who was Stokely Carmichael?

Stokely Carmichael first emerged in the civil rights movement as a 19-year-old Freedom Rider. By 1963 he was a well-known member of the SNCC. In that year he began to disagree with members of the SNCC and other civil rights leaders about non-violent protest. He wanted stronger action against the white racist violence and he also wanted more black Americans to be able to vote easily. In that sense, Stokely Carmichael had the same aims as the non-violent section of the civil rights movement. However, the split in the civil rights movement was made even more obvious when Carmichael, then leader of the SNCC, changed the meaning of the 'N' in its name from 'non-violent' to 'national'. By the mid-1960s, many black Americans no longer believed that non-violence was the way forward. They looked towards 'Black Power' for help.

What was Black Power?

Some critics of Stokely Carmichael said that the 'Black Power' slogan was racist and too simple. All it did, said his critics, was to make people angry and violent. On the other hand, many young black Americans living in the ghettos were attracted to the Black Power movement by Carmichael's more extreme, aggressive message, summed up when he said:

The only way we gonna stop them white men from whippin' us is to take over. We been sayin' freedom for six years and we ain't got nothin'. What we gonna start sayin' now is Black Power.

Stokely Carmichael explained that 'Black Power' meant black Americans taking control of their political and economic future. He said that black Americans should not rely on white people to 'give' them civil rights and that white support for the civil rights movement was not wanted. He said, 'I am not going to beg the white man for anything I deserve. I'm going to take it.' He argued that black Americans should build up their own schools, communities, businesses, even hospitals, without interference from whites.

This was all very different from the style and ideas of Martin Luther King Jr and, by 1966, the idea of Black Power had become established as an alternative to King's non-violent protest methods.

How relevant was the civil rights campaign to northern black Americans?

While Martin Luther King Jr had concentrated on civil rights issues in the southern states, new ideas and new leaders were growing in the northern cities.

The campaign in the South to end segregation and discrimination was more or less over. However, the problems of black Americans in the main cities of the North had hardly been touched.

By 1965, half of all black Americans lived in the cities of the North and West. Most of them lived in slum areas that were known as ghettos. They had to live with poor housing, high rents, unemployment, poverty and hunger. Gang violence and drug-related crime were also increasing. Faced with these problems, many black Americans in the cities were attracted to the ideas of the Nation of Islam.

'The Architect of Black Power'

Who is this? Use two clues in the picture as evidence. Why do you think the editor of this magazine chose to use this picture?

What were the beliefs of the Nation of Islam?

The Nation of Islam, also known as the Black Muslims, was founded in Detroit, Michigan in 1930 and was led by Elijah Muhammad. It supported the creation of a separate black nation on the US mainland, separate from white society in every way – economically, politically and spiritually.

The Nation of Islam attracted many black Americans with its ideas of strict moral discipline, respect for religious faith and apparent ability to 'straighten out' the lives of many individuals such as drug addicts and criminals who had been considered beyond hope. One of those 'saved' souls was Malcolm X.

Who was Malcolm X?

Malcolm Little was a petty criminal who was converted to the Nation of Islam while in prison and changed his name to Malcolm X. He claimed that his surname of 'Little' was a white name given to his family by slave owners many years before, so the 'X' referred to his unknown African name. Until he and his followers rediscovered their African names, they would use letters as their last names, representing their stolen identities.

Malcolm X was a very different black leader compared to Martin Luther King Jr. The Nation of Islam completely rejected the integration ideas of people such as King. Malcolm X criticised King's non-violent appeals by saying:

The goal of Dr King is to give Negroes a chance to sit in a segregated restaurant beside the same white folks who have persecuted, beaten and lynched black people for years. Dr King seems to want black people to forgive the people who have beaten, bought, sold, and lynched our people for 400 years.

Malcolm X became a preacher for the Nation of Islam and spoke out against King's belief in non-violence. He declared that non-violence was another word for being defenceless and he clearly rejected the aims and methods of King. Malcolm X believed that the USA's claim to be a land of the free was false and applied only to white people. He rejected help from whites and stated that black Americans needed to work out their own futures without relying on white help. Malcolm X was one of the first black activists to draw attention to the increasing problems within the ghettos of American cities: crime, prostitution, drugs and unemployment.

Malcolm X warned that if nothing were done, violence would erupt in the USA's cities. He was right!

'Nobody can give you freedom. Nobody can give you equality or justice or anything. If you're a man, you take it.'

How do the words with this picture of Malcolm X illustrate one of the core disagreements with the non-violent approach of Martin Luther King Jr?

What were the Black Panthers?

While the Nation of Islam was strong in New York and the north-eastern cities of the USA, another black radical group was growing on the west coast. The Black Panther Party for Self-Defence was founded in October 1966 in Oakland, California by Huey P. Newton and Bobby Seale. The Black Panthers represented the complete opposite of Martin Luther King Jr's ideas and supported the anti-white, black **separatist** ideas of Stokely Carmichael and Malcolm X. The Panthers were prepared to use violence in order to achieve their

GLOSSARY

Separatist relating to racial and cultural separation

goals and saw the police as the enemy of black communities. When Black Panther leaders explained their ideas, they stated many of the complaints of the USA's black population. Their demands included full employment for all, better housing which was 'fit for the shelter of human beings', honest education, an end to police brutality and fair trials with black juries for black people.

Why did the Black Panthers choose that name?

Huey P. Newton explained that the name 'Black Panther' was chosen because the panther is a strong fighter when it is cornered and will protect its family. Black Panther leaders spoke about using violence to protect black communities against white violence. According to Newton, their most important demand was an immediate end to police brutality and the murder of black people. He also said that Panther patrols should carry guns on the streets of US cities so that they could protect their 'brothers' (other black people). He said:

What good was non-violence when the police were determined to rule by force? Out on patrol we stopped whenever we saw the police questioning a brother or sister. We would observe from a safe distance so that the police could not say we were interfering with the performance of their duty. We were checking out the police.

The Black Panther Party became very popular among young black Americans who lived in the big cities. By the summer of 1968 a branch of the Black Panthers had been established in most US cities.

Were Black Panthers only interested in violence?

The Black Panthers were usually shown on television and in magazines in deliberately threatening poses, wearing black leather jackets, black berets and dark glasses, and carrying guns.

What was not so well publicised were the self-help programmes launched by the Black Panthers in their own communities. Panthers not only talked about 'serving the people', they also had a policy of doing things to help improve life in the ghettos. They organised community programmes such as free breakfasts for children, free health clinics, local school support groups, free clothes for the poor and campaigns to stop drugs and crime in black areas of US cities.

Why did the Black Panthers choose to use this poster for publicity? If you were a white newspaper editor using this poster what captions might you use to go with it? Think of several.

'The racist dog policemen must withdraw immediately from our communities, cease their wanton murder and brutality and torture of black people, or face the wrath of the armed people.'

How important were the Black Panthers?

The deliberately threatening poses in the self-publicity of the Black Panthers grabbed headlines at a time when much of white society was afraid of black protest movements. However, even at their height, the Black Panthers only had 2000 members.

Public attention was distracted by the riots erupting in cities all across the USA and the Black Panthers were thought to be just a small part of the violence sweeping over the country in the late 1960s.

What happened to the Black Panthers?

The Panthers were the most violent group to emerge in the late 1960s but by 1969, 27 Panthers were dead and over 700 were in prison. By 1970 the more violent of the Black Panther leaders were either dead or in prison. Many black Americans realised that all the riots did was destroy black property and kill black people.

The Black Panther Party lost its influence when quarrels among its leaders broke out. By the middle of the 1970s the Black Panther Party no longer existed.

How did federal authority react to the black radical groups?

By the mid-1960s federal authorities worried about protest groups generally. The USA was involved in an unpopular war in **Vietnam** and there were increasing protests about it at home. This was also a time of youth protest and thousands of young people in their teens and twenties were rebelling against the rules of an older generation. The civil rights movement seemed to have made real gains with new federal laws in place – and then riots broke out in the big cities.

The president, federal authorities and state governors all became worried that there was some sort of plot to take over the USA.

Why did the federal government see Malcolm X as a threat?

Malcolm X became a very powerful preacher. His message of self-help attracted many listeners who were tired of having to wait on white authority to improve conditions. Malcolm X also spoke of a separate nation for black Americans only.

The US government was afraid that Malcolm X was building up hatred against whites that could erupt in national riots and revolution. Already there had been riots in Los Angeles, California. The white authorities were afraid that these riots would spread as more and more black Americans were attracted to the Nation of Islam, more commonly known as the Black Muslims.

Malcolm X left the Black Muslims after serious arguments with the Elijah Muhammad and Malcolm was warned by other followers that there was a plot to kill him. Probably as a result of his falling out with Elijah Muhammad, Malcolm X's home was firebombed and a week later he was murdered while giving a speech. The three gunmen were linked to the Nation of Islam but there was suspicion that the FBI was also involved.

How did federal authority react to black radical groups such as the Black Panthers?

The head of the FBI, J. Edgar Hoover, told his agents that they should cause as many arguments and splits within the Black Panther Party as possible. He went on to ask FBI officers to plan ways of destroying the Black Panther Party.

During the 1960s, the FBI spied on many black leaders. When **black radicals** became more violent, the FBI increased its activities to undermine and weaken black organisations. The FBI called its targets 'Black Nationalist Hate Groups'. Memos sent to FBI agents told them to disrupt the meetings of any black protest group and especially to prevent the rise of any black leader who would unify the various protest organisations.

The FBI also tried to make black organisations look bad in order to stop the growth of any white support for the protest groups. For example, FBI action was used to destroy the positive work of the Black Panthers such as the free breakfast programme. FBI agents were used to make it difficult to sell the party's newspaper and to disrupt local education classes run by the Black Panthers.

While the FBI said it was protecting law and order, many others said the FBI was taking away basic freedoms in the USA, such as the right to support the political ideas you agree with and the right to print newspapers which may or may not support the government.

> ### GLOSSARY
> **Black radicals** black Americans, mainly in cities, who rejected non-violent protest in favour of violence to make changes in the ghettos

Activity 1

Wordsearch

Get a copy or make your own version of the wordbox shown here.

Use the wordsearch grid to hide five main words, names or ideas linked in some way with black radical groups. Complete the grid with random letters to conceal your words. Do not show where the words are on your grid. Your partner must find them. So, what you do is write definitions of the words below or beside your wordsearch.

When you have completed your wordsearch puzzle, exchange with your partner. Read their clues and find the word. As they solve your puzzle, you solve theirs.

Activity 2

The challenge! How far can you go?

The following questions go up in level of difficulty in pairs. The first two are easy. The last two are hard. How many will you try to do?

1 List three black radical leaders and describe their ideas.
2 What were the problems of the ghettos that made many black Americans support radical groups?

3 Why do you think white magazines usually showed pictures of black radical leaders looking angry or threatening?
4 How would you summarise the attitudes of many white people in the USA to black radicals?

5 What information would you use to support the view that black radicals were unfairly shown as violent and aggressive in the media?
6 Give arguments for and against the reaction of the federal authorities to black radicals.

Activity 3

Project task

Create a presentation or display about the black radical groups that grew up in the USA in the 1960s. How you present or display this information is entirely up to you. You can choose to work on your own or as part of a group no larger than four. If you work in a group, you must also design and use a creativity log in which you record exactly what each person in the group contributed to the final presentation or display.

Success criteria

▶ Your presentation or display must explain what the black radicals were.
▶ It must contain details of three different leaders.
▶ It must give at least two examples of black radical groups.
▶ It must contain at least one illustration for each group.
▶ The presentation or display must be clear, colourful and informative.
▶ If it is a presentation, it should last between two and four minutes.
▶ If it is a display it should be at least A2 size (that's twice the size of A3).
▶ The information must be relevant and accurate.

Question practice

Source A was said by a young black girl living in a ghetto in Chicago in 1966.

SOURCE A

During a protest march in Mississippi we first heard the phrase 'Black Power'. We immediately supported it because we were tired of waiting on changes in the law. We wanted a better life now.

Explain why young black Americans supported the slogan 'Black Power'.

Success criteria

In your answer you should include at least two points of information about why young black Americans were attracted by the Black Power slogan.

Source A is from a television interview with Malcolm X where he spoke of his ideas about civil rights.

SOURCE A

Our people have made the mistake of confusing the methods with the objectives. As long as we agree on objectives, we should never fall out with each other just because we believe in different methods, or tactics, or strategy. We have to keep in mind at all times that we are not fighting to be different from each other. We are fighting for recognition as free humans in this society.

Evaluate the usefulness of Source A as evidence of the black radical groups in the USA in the 1960s. **(5 marks)**

You need to make five clear points about the usefulness of the source. You would probably start by arguing that the source does provide useful evidence about the black radical groups. You could mention:

▶ When the source was written and why that makes it useful in terms of the question.
▶ Who the speaker of the source was and why that makes it useful in terms of the question.
▶ How the content of the source makes it useful in terms of the question.

You should also explain the limitations of the source by explaining what the source does not tell us and why that makes it useful in terms of the question.

Chapter 15 The problem of the ghettos

What is this chapter about?

Between 1950 and 1960, four million black Americans had migrated from the South looking for homes and jobs in the northern cities. By 1965, half of all black Americans lived in the cities of the North and West. However, much of the black population lived in run down, slum areas of the cities. These slum areas were known as ghettos. Martin Luther King Jr was aware of the growing black radical protests and the discontent in the urban ghettos. As a result, King and his followers moved North to attack the problems of the cities.

By the end of this chapter you should be able to:

▶ Describe the problems facing black Americans in the major cities of the North.
▶ Explain why the Kerner Commission report shocked the USA.
▶ Decide if black Americans could really claim to be 'free at last' in 1968.

How relevant was the civil rights campaign to black Americans in northern cities of the USA?

You will remember that many immigrants from Europe had lived in ghettos when they first arrived in the USA. Usually, within a generation, the immigrant families had saved enough money to move out of the ghettos. However, as black Americans moved into ghetto areas, they found the colour of their skin was an added difficulty in the struggle to escape. The problem of racial discrimination and prejudice was added to the difficulties of breaking out of the vicious cycle of poverty.

By 1965, half of all black Americans lived in the cities of the North and West. Most of them lived in the slum areas that were known as ghettos. They had to live with poor housing, high rents, unemployment, poverty and hunger. Urban gang violence and drug-associated crime were also increasing.

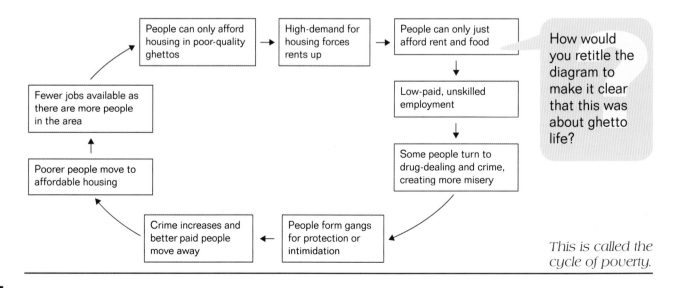

How would you retitle the diagram to make it clear that this was about ghetto life?

This is called the cycle of poverty.

For many young black Americans in the cities, the civil rights movement of the 1950s and early 1960s was an irrelevance. The protestors in the cities agreed that they could ride on the same buses, eat in the same restaurants and even live in the same districts as white people, but without jobs and money what real benefits had the civil rights campaign brought them?

What happened in the Watts district of Los Angeles in 1965?

In 1965, a riot erupted in the Watts district of Los Angeles, California. It was the first of several riots that broke out in many US cities between 1964 and 1967. Ninety-eight per cent of the population of the Watts district in Los Angeles was black, but the police force was almost entirely white. The combination of a long hot summer, poverty, unemployment and violent police action sparked off a riot that lasted for six days and left 34 people dead, 900 wounded and 4000 arrested. Fourteen thousand troops were required to restore order but none of the causes of the riot were dealt with.

A crowd confronts an armed National Guardsman.

The Watts riot showed that Martin Luther King Jr was no longer the leader of a united civil rights movement. When King went to Los Angeles to try to spread a non-violent message, young black Americans heckled and shouted at him. Black Americans in the big cities were no longer attracted to King's message of non-violence.

The importance of the Watts riot, and others that followed, was to show that poverty, hunger, poor housing and unemployment were far more important to black people in the cities than the 'older' civil rights issues of desegregation and voting rights in the South.

The problems of the urban ghettos marked a major turning point in the campaign for civil rights. Some historians say that King lost his focus and the city problems were just too big for him. Others argue that King's message of non-violence was no longer popular and the more violent message of Black Power promised quicker results. However, the city of Chicago asked King to help.

Why did King want to go to Chicago?

Urban riots in 1965 convinced King that Chicago had become the symbol of the race problem in northern cities. King believed that if he could make a difference there, support for his message would be revived. King selected segregated housing as the main issue for the focus of his protest. However, tensions in Chicago went deeper than the issue of housing.

Chicago got hotter and hotter in the summer of 1966. On 12 July police closed a fire hydrant that had been opened by black teenagers wanting to cool down. A fight broke out. Ten people were injured, windows were smashed and some shops looted. The mayor dismissed it as unimportant kids' crime. Martin Luther King Jr called it a riot. On the next night, sniper fire, petrol bombs and the stoning of city firefighters seemed to support King's description.

What was the importance of the Chicago riot?

King faced difficulties in Chicago. The tactics that had been successful in Birmingham would not work here. Chicago was not a southern town with southern issues of segregation and local politicians unaware of the power of the media. The mayor of Chicago was Richard Daley, a powerful politician who knew how to handle the media and how to cope with opposition to his policies. Mayor Daley made some vague promises to King about improvements in housing but these promises were not kept. Far from restoring his credibility in the civil rights campaign, the Chicago protest weakened King's influence. Many people were more attracted to calls for Black Power.

Why did President Johnson create the Kerner Commission?

In 1966 there were another 43 'race riots' but despite extra government money for schools, housing, jobs and health programmes, the looting, rioting and killing continued. Civil rights leaders condemned the violence but young black Americans refused to listen. One of the most destructive riots was in Detroit. Several people were killed and millions of dollars' worth of property was destroyed.

After the Detroit riot, President **Lyndon B. Johnson** asked **Otto Kerner**, who was then governor of the state of Illinois, to investigate thoroughly the causes of the urban riots.

The task of the **Kerner Commission** was to investigate the real causes of the urban riots. President Johnson suspected that a minority of people was using the urban problems as an excuse to start a revolution in the USA. He did not believe the riots were a genuine reaction of people who felt they had no other option but to riot.

GLOSSARY

Lyndon B. Johnson president of the USA after Kennedy's assassination

Otto Kerner governor of Illinois and chairman of the Kerner Commission

Kerner Commission set up by the US president to investigate the 1967 race riots

How would you react to this photo if you were a white American? How would you react if you were black and living in a Detroit ghetto?

A photo published in a magazine about the Detroit riots.

Why was the Kerner Commission's report so important?

When the Kerner Commission made its report public in 1968, Americans were shocked by what it said. Kerner was white and he had no reason to make excuses for black rioters. Kerner did not agree with President Johnson and said that the problems of the urban ghettos were not caused by outside troublemakers. The problems of the ghettos were caused by genuine poverty that was the result of the lack of opportunities for black Americans to improve their lives. In fact, Kerner claimed the riots were caused by a white society that did not seem to care about black Americans.

Kerner reported that 40 per cent of all black Americans lived in poverty and that the riots and other crimes were caused by poverty. Kerner stated that black men were twice as likely to be unemployed as white men and that black men were three times as likely to be in low-skilled jobs.

The Kerner Commission concluded that:

our nation is moving towards two societies, one black, one white – separate and unequal.

The Kerner Commission's report went on to say that white society created the ghettos, white society kept them going and white society did nothing to improve them. The Kerner Commission reminded the USA that it was still a long way from being a free and equal society.

Did the assassination of Martin Luther King Jr mark the end of the civil rights campaigns?

King knew his influence was slipping away. Despite increasing pressure to change his ideas to attract new support, King stuck to what he believed in. He intended to show the USA that he could still use non-violent protest to improve people's lives, but on 4 April 1968, Martin Luther King Jr was shot and killed as he stood on his motel balcony in Memphis, Tennessee. When word spread of his death, riots erupted in 168 cities. It took 70,000 troops to restore order. It seemed that the non-violent civil rights movement had died with King.

What did Martin Luther King Jr achieve?

Martin Luther King Jr was a charismatic leader who knew how to use the relatively new medium of television to gain public sympathy and to put pressure on the federal authority. He helped to make changes so that life in the USA, especially in the South, was very different in 1965 to what it had been in 1955. Even Stokely Carmichael said that King was the one man who the masses of black Americans would listen to. Nearly every black American, and most whites, agreed that King was one of the most important leaders of any colour in the twentieth century. Today, King remains an icon representing dignified protest against unjust conditions and unfair treatment of human beings.

Martin Luther King Jr was killed on a motel balcony. How did this news seem to represent the end of an era?

1968: 'Free at last?'

In 1968, King was dead. That same year, the world was reminded of the civil rights issue at the Mexico Olympic Games when two black American runners mounted the rostrum to receive their medals. The USA was shocked and embarrassed by what happened next. As the US flag was raised and the national anthem was played, the two athletes, John Carlos and Tommie Smith, dropped their heads and refused to look at the flag. They raised one arm, with a black-gloved clenched fist, in a Black Power salute. It was a message that some black Americans did not feel they belonged to the USA and that the athletes were supporters of Black Power.

> What impression did the world get of race relations in the USA in 1968 when they saw this event on television? Do you think it was a fair impression?

Black American athletes give a Black Power salute at the 1968 Mexico Olympics.

> Explain what point the photographer was trying to make. Why has this image been included at the end of this book?

> Describe, in detail, exactly what this picture shows.

This course is called 'Free at Last?' and ends in 1968. The question mark in the title is important. The title is not stating that black Americans were free at last in 1968. It is asking how far black Americans were free by 1968. In other words, how successful had the civil rights campaigns been? In 1968 it seemed that the USA was still divided over race.

Activity 1

If this is the answer what is the question?

Below you will find a list of words or names. You have to make up a question that can only be answered by the word on the list. For example, if the word 'Daley' was the answer, a question could be 'who was the Mayor of Chicago in 1966?'

- ghetto
- the cycle of poverty
- Watts, Los Angeles
- Detroit
- Otto Kerner
- outside troublemakers
- Mexico
- Black Power salute
- President Johnson.

Activity 2

Your cycle of poverty

Look at the cycle of poverty diagram on page 94 very carefully for 30 seconds. Then close the book. From memory, draw your own version of the cycle of poverty. Your points must connect and your version must be colourful and informative. You are not asked to copy or repeat the cycle exactly. Your version could be a simplified version but make the same points that one problem links to the next and it is very difficult to escape. Your version should have appropriate illustrations.

Activity 3

This is a National 4 activity

How did the civil rights movement improve life for black Americans between 1960 and 1968?

Your task is to use the historical information in this chapter and anything else you can discover to design a display or make a presentation about something important in the civil rights movement between 1960 and 1968.

Your display or presentation should show the main events and the key people involved in the movement. There are various ways you can design this. A few ideas are listed below.

- You may wish to create an information poster divided into 'non-violent protest' and 'black radical' protest.
- Or, you could present the information in the form of a leaflet, a mind-map or a storyboard that details the story of the civil rights movement between 1960 and 1968.
- There may also be an opportunity for you to design a slideshow presentation that can be shared with the class or saved on your school's website for revision.

You can produce your own images or you can print off images from the internet to cut out and stick on to your information poster to make a collage.

It is important to remember that you will only be assessed on your historical understanding and not on the artistic qualities of your display or presentation. However, it should be presented in a clear and neat manner to allow your audience to fully understand your main ideas.

Activity 4

This is a National 5 activity. Design a revision mobile

You have a choice of two activities:

▶ design a mobile illustrating the development of the civil rights movement from 1945 to 1968 *or*

▶ design a mobile explaining the black radical movement in the USA in the late 1960s.

You can choose to work on your own or as part of a group no larger than four. If you work in a group, you must also design and use a creativity log in which you record exactly what each person in the group contributed to the final mobile.

Success criteria

▶ Your mobile must have at least four strands.

▶ Each strand should be about a main theme in the civil rights or black radical movement.

▶ Each strand should have several mobile items attached.

▶ Each strand must have at least two text items, each containing significant names or words.

▶ Each strand must have at least one large, double-sided illustration linked to an event or personality.

▶ Each strand must have a three-dimensional feature that represents a major event in its strand.

▶ Your mobile should hang easily.

▶ Your mobile must be able to be read from a distance.

▶ Your mobile must be attractive, colourful and relevant to the project task.

Question practice

National 4

Source A is from a Black Power supporter in Chicago, 1968.

SOURCE A

By the summer of 1966 Stokely Carmichael's call for Black Power had reached Chicago. King wanted to keep Black Power quiet but he knew nothing about our lives in the cities. We wanted to shout Black Power from the rooftops!

Source B is from a black shopkeeper in Detroit, 1968.

SOURCE B

Martin Luther King did a lot of good work in the South but up here in the cities he just does not know what problems we face day to day. We got no segregation or Jim Crow here. What we got here is no jobs, families in poverty and bad, bad housing. What's Martin Luther King gonna do about that?

Compare the views in Source A and Source B about Martin Luther King Jr. Describe in detail their similarities and/or differences. You can also briefly compare the overall attitude of the sources.

Success criteria

▶ Examine the two sources in order to show two simple points of comparison or one developed point of similarity or difference.
▶ A simple comparison: 'Source A says … and Source B says …' will get 1 mark.
▶ A developed comparison: 'Sources A and B agree about attitudes towards Martin Luther King Jr and his relevance to the race issues in the big cities of the North. The evidence is that Source A says … and Source B says …' will get 2 marks.

Now make another comparison connection.

National 5

To what extent did the black radical protests fail to achieve their aims? **(8 marks)**

There is no source provided for a 'to what extent' question. You will only get one 'to what extent' question in your entire National 5 exam paper. To be successful in this type of question you need to decide how important a particular factor was in explaining why something happened. In this case, you are asked how successful the black radical groups were in achieving their aims. You must come up with at least five points and organise them into a balanced answer. You will then give a short conclusion that sums up your answer to the question.

Glossary

A

Airbrush – a way of making something vanish from sight in a photograph

Amendment – a change or alteration

American dream – the hope that everyone could be happy and successful in the USA

Anarchism – the destruction of all government, law and order

Arkansas – a state in the South – Little Rock is its capital city

Assassinated – murdered for political reasons

Assembly line – factory work where workers only do one simple task in a long process

Assimilation – mixing together to become like everyone else in the USA

B

The Birth of a Nation – an influential film released in 1915

Black radicals – black Americans, mainly in cities, who rejected non-violent protest in favour of violence to make changes in the ghettos

Bolshevism – Communism

Boycott – to deliberately stop doing something to create pressure for change

C

Civil disobedience – deliberately refusing to obey laws

Civil rights – everyone in a country should be treated the same

Communism – a political belief that society should be classless, which sparked off the Russian revolution

Congress – like the UK Parliament, it makes laws

D

Deep South – states in the USA which are the furthest from the North, such as Alabama and Georgia

Discrimination – unfair treatment

Double jeopardy – a law which states that a person cannot be put on trial for the same crime more than once

E

Eisenhower, Dwight – President of the USA in 1957

Endowed – to be given something

Eugenics – a belief that one race of people is genetically better than another

Exclusion – keeping people out of the USA

F

Faubus, Orval – the Arkansas state governor in 1957

FBI – Federal Bureau of Investigation, the US federal detective agency

Federal – national government of the USA

Federal authority – the national government of the USA

Freedom Rides – travelling on buses to check and challenge racial segregation

Funtown – a theme park that black children could not go to

G

Ghettos – areas of cities that had bad housing. They attracted black Americans because this housing was cheap

Grand Wizard of the Empire – the title of the Ku Klux Klan leader

Great Migration – the movement of black Americans from the South to northern cities around the First World War

H

Hindsight – looking back on events and thinking you know better than the people at the time

I

Immigrants – people who arrived in a new country to create new lives for themselves

Inalienable – something that cannot be taken away

Interstate – connections between US states

Invisible Empire – the official title of the Ku Klux Klan

J

Jim Crow – the name used to describe laws made after the US Civil War to segregate black and white Americans

Johnson, Lyndon B. – president of the USA after Kennedy's assassination

K

Kennedy, John F. – president of the USA from 1960 until his assassination in 1963

Kerner Commission – set up by the US president to investigate the 1967 race riots

Kerner, Otto – governor of Illinois and chairman of the Kerner Commission

L

Legislation – new laws

Lincoln Memorial – a monument to President Lincoln, who had been assassinated in 1865. He was the president who had ended slavery in the USA

Lynching – the illegal murder of someone, usually by a mob and usually for a racial reason

M

Mafia – organised crime gangs that began in Sicily, Italy

Melting pot – the hope that different nationalities would develop a new identity: an American one

N

NAACP – National Association for the Advancement of Coloured People – a civil rights organisation

National Guard – a state-controlled military force made up of part-time members

Nativism – a belief that ideas and people from outside the USA were bad

Nordics – people from northern Europe

O

Open door – a policy of allowing anyone to come and live in the USA

P

Patriotic – loving or supporting your country

Poll tax – a local tax, the payment of which was often used as evidence that people were entitled to vote

Prohibition – a time in the 1920s when the USA tried to ban the sale of all alcohol

Project C – the name of the protest campaign launched by the civil rights movement in Birmingham

R

Racism – treating people differently because of the colour of their skin

Radical – wanting fast change, sometimes with violence

Red – Communist

S

Segregation – keeping black and while people apart

Separate but equal – a phrase used in a decision of the Supreme Court in 1896 that made segregation legal and respectable across the USA

Separatist – relating to racial and cultural separation

Sheriff – the chief of the local police

Sit-in – a non-violent protest of blocking an area by remaining seated

SNCC – Student Non-violent Co-ordinating Committee, a civil rights group

Sterilisation – a medical procedure to stop women from being able to have children. Sometimes done against the will of the woman

T

Topeka – a town in Kansas, USA

U

Urban – anything to do with being in a city

US Constitution – the basic rules about how the USA is governed and the rights of American people

V

Vietnam – a country in South-east Asia that the USA was trying to prevent from becoming Communist

Voter registration – in the USA all people with the right to vote must register before they can cast their vote

W

Wasp – White Anglo-Saxon Protestant

Index